What people are saying about

Why an Afterlife Obviously Exists

Like a master attorney, Jens Amberts has marshaled an abundance of virtually irrefutable evidence in making the case for the thesis of his brilliant book, *Why an Afterlife Obviously Exists*. Basing his argument on four fundamental facts about near-death experiences (NDEs), Amberts has written a book that every serious student of NDEs, and especially skeptics, should be sure to read. On finishing it, I doubt any reader will not be convinced that death is not a dead end.

Kenneth Ring, Ph.D., Professor Emeritus of Psychology, University of Connecticut, author of *Lessons from the Light*

Jens Amberts has written a book unlike any other. *Why an Afterlife Obviously Exists* argues that the testimony of near-death experiencers estab' s beyond any reasonable doubt that we do survive th. Furthermore, it presents an impressive lo all of us should take that testimony se nversational style that is easily ac ook is one that deserves to be read, Amberts presents arguments that you w long after you have finished reading his book.

Bruce Gre M.D., Professor Emeritus of Psychiatry & Neurobehavioral Sciences, University of Virginia, author of *After: A Doctor Explores What Near-Death Experiences Reveal About Life and Beyond*

What happens when we die has been one of humankind's most enduring questions. *Why an Afterlife Obviously Exists* brings a new and exciting perspective to this ancient question. Jens

Amberts presents an impressive discussion of the evidence for the reality of near-death experiences (NDEs). This includes an original and creative thought experiment that is among the most compelling verifications of the validity of NDEs and their consistent message of an afterlife that I have encountered. This is one book you don't want to miss! *Why an Afterlife Obviously Exists* is exceptionally well-written and enthusiastically recommended.

Jeffrey Long, M.D., author of the *New York Times* bestselling *Evidence of the Afterlife: The Science of Near-Death Experiences*

Jens Amberts' *Why an Afterlife Obviously Exists* is a breath of fresh air in the world of academic philosophy. He tackles a question of supreme existential importance and makes a careful and convincing case that there exists a world more comprehensive and compellingly real than the one of which we are currently aware. This book deserves not only to be widely read but to have its conclusions considered with the utmost seriousness.

Sharon Hewitt Rawlette, Ph.D., author of *The Source and Significance of Coincidences* and the *Psychology Today* blog "Mysteries of Consciousness"

Through a carefully-crafted philosophical argument, Amberts documents the empirical and rational basis for his own transformation from a philosophical materialist – believing that the material world is the only reality – to a survivalist – convinced that another reality exists, one in which human consciousness continues after physical death. This book is a must-read for any truly open-minded empiricist interested in the question of the most accurate view of the cosmos.

Janice Miner Holden, Ed.D., editor-in-chief of the *Journal of Near-Death Studies*, co-author of *The Handbook of Near-Death Experiences: Thirty Years of Investigation*

The fear of death has probably caused more suffering in the history of the human race than all the physical diseases combined. Jens Amberts, in *Why an Afterlife Obviously Exists*, offers compelling reasons why this fear and suffering may be exaggerated and unnecessary. Amberts' fresh voice is subtle, profound, and reminiscent of philosopher Michele de Montaigne, who assured us, "If you don't know how to die, don't worry; Nature will tell you what to do on the spot, fully and adequately. She will do this job perfectly for you; don't bother your head about it." *Why an Afterlife Obviously Exists* is a richly rewarding adventure in ideas.

Larry Dossey, M.D., author most recently of *One Mind: How Our Individual Mind Is Part of a Greater Consciousness and Why It Matters*

Based on scientific research and on intriguing reports of near-death experiences (NDE), this book *Why an Afterlife Obviously Exists* gives a very nice overview and summary of what can be learned about the afterlife, or, even better, about the continuity of consciousness after the death of the body. People with an NDE are convinced that death is not the end of our consciousness, and they are all forced to change their existing worldview. Jens Amberts uses an interesting analogy to better understand and accept the conclusions that during an NDE the content of our consciousness is experienced far more real than the reality we know in the material world of everyday life. This book has been written for those open-minded readers who are genuinely interested in the possibility of the continuity of consciousness after physical death.

Pim van Lommel, cardiologist, NDE-researcher, author of *Consciousness Beyond Life*

Why an Afterlife Obviously Exists

A Thought Experiment and Realer Than
Real Near-Death Experiences

Why an Afterlife Obviously Exists

A Thought Experiment and Realer Than
Real Near-Death Experiences

Jens Amberts

IFF
BOOKS

Winchester, UK
Washington, USA

JOHN HUNT PUBLISHING

First published by iff Books, 2022
iff Books is an imprint of John Hunt Publishing Ltd., No. 3 East Street, Alresford,
Hampshire SO24 9EE, UK
office@jhpbooks.com
www.johnhuntpublishing.com
www.iff-books.com

For distributor details and how to order please visit the 'Ordering' section on our website.

Text copyright: Jens Amberts 2021

ISBN: 978 1 78535 985 9
978 1 78904 410 2 (ebook)
Library of Congress Control Number: 2020942477

A CIP catalogue record for this book is available from the British Library.

Design: Stuart Davies

UK: Printed and bound by CPI Group (UK) Ltd, Croydon, CR0 4YY
Printed in North America by CPI GPS partners

We operate a distinctive and ethical publishing philosophy in
all areas of our business, from our global network of authors to
production and worldwide distribution.

Contents

This book is dedicated to all of humanity for all time to come.

Preface

This is a book about four things divided into three different main chapters. One chapter concerns a new thought experiment in philosophy. Another chapter concerns an in-depth and arguably trailblazing analysis of the realer than real attribute of near-death experiences (NDEs). The last major chapter concerns a clarification of what to some have been previously considered at least somewhat ambiguous data about NDEs. And the fourth overarching and permeating thing is how all of this ties together to demonstrate why it is beyond astronomically likely and hence empirically certain that an afterlife actually exists.

The argument in this book became evident to me soon after I started researching NDEs seriously back in 2006 and 2007, as it does to many others as well who start researching NDEs. However, most researchers and thinkers have so far not pressed this issue when arguing whether an afterlife exists or not. But since as far as I can tell and judge the situation it is the single most convincing argument in favor of the existence of an afterlife, I have therefore decided to press this issue myself. So in 2016 when I one day spontaneously came up with a thought experiment that made it so much easier to articulate this argument as clearly as I have now done, I began writing this book. It was first intended to become a peer-reviewed article, but as I kept on writing and expanding the text greatly, it eventually became too long to fit in the vast majority of peer-reviewed philosophy journals. Hence I decided to make a book of it instead.

In general, there are three potential ways of being justifiably certain that an afterlife exists. These are to either have a personal experience of it, or to be persuaded by scientific data indicative of it, or to be persuaded by philosophical arguments in favor of it. Since the reading of any book can never become the first reason, neither is the reading of this book. But it is presenting a philosophical argument that is based on four non-controversial empirical facts about NDEs, so it is a combination of the latter two reasons. I chose to write this book for many reasons, but one of them was because I want to give the rest of the world a chance to be and feel as justifiably certain of the existence of an afterlife as I am, despite the fact that most people have never had an unambiguously direct experience of the afterlife themselves (and this also includes me). The reality is, after all, that most people who do not believe in an afterlife do not do so because they have never experienced it or anything even slightly indicative of it directly themselves. But we do not have to experience something directly ourselves to justifiably know that it exists. I have experienced neither Australia nor the planet Neptune directly myself, but I can still justifiably know that these places exist based on many other considerations and inferences. And while the title of this book states that it is obvious that an afterlife exists, obviously it is not as obvious that an afterlife exists as, say, that the sky appears as blue on a sunny and cloudless day. Books, scientific data, and philosophical arguments are ultimately just words on paper or on a screen, and they can only ever convince a person on an intellectual level of something, and not on an experiential level. But it is obvious enough from an intellectual level when you familiarize yourself with and reflect upon the argument presented in this book that an afterlife in all likelihood actually exists, such that it will be very hard to rationally deny it. So in this book I will guide you through a lot of considerations and inferences to demonstrate why you can feel and be justifiably certain that an afterlife exists, despite never having experienced it yourself. Indeed, the argument being presented in this book is central to the discussion of whether an afterlife exists or not and can no longer be ignored or downplayed while preserving intellectual honesty and responsibility in the pursuit of truth on the matter.

Jens Amberts, Linköping, 2021

Acknowledgements

We are all greatly helped by the insights and work of those who came before us. And we are also often helped to achieve what we set out to do in life by the love and support of our friends and family members who act as the wind beneath our wings. And this is no exception. This book could never have been written without near-death experiencers (NDErs) having the courage to come forward with and share their testimonies. Special mention to NDErs Howard Storm, Christian Andréason, Nanci Danison, and Nicole Swann, whose extensive testimonies have greatly shaped my own understanding of near-death experiences (NDEs). Furthermore, this book could not have been written without the prior work of the many NDE researchers who over many decades by now have greatly enriched our understanding of NDEs. Special mention to the philosophers Neal Grossman, Chris Carter, and Keith Augustine for greatly influencing my own understanding and thinking about NDEs with their insightful writings. Lastly, special mention on a personal level to Johan Nordlund, Anders Holmström, David Santiago Carrión, Pernilla Hokkanen, and Micaela Crane, as well as my other friends and family members, including, of course, my beloved mother Yvonne Bengtsson for her endless support, love, understanding, and acceptance of me wanting if not outright needing to forge my own life story and walk the path less traveled in life.

Chapter 1

Introduction

There is arguably no question that is more important for humanity as a whole, or for the average individual, than the question of whether an afterlife exists or not. And it is definitely granted that very many people already believe, hope, or doubt that an afterlife exists. But belief, hope, or doubt does not really take us very far, or rather, it results in the kind of world we live in right now with respect to this issue, where everyone has different viewpoints, beliefs, opinions, and doubts. In this book, however, I will make the case that we already know, with a high degree of certainty, that an afterlife exists, if we reflect upon four non-controversial facts about the near-death experience (NDE) in a new light and from a more philosophical perspective. Unfortunately, however, the question of whether an afterlife exists or not is all too often not merely a factual, rational, and empirical question for ideologically stubborn and emotional human beings who do not live in a cultural vacuum. It is not as neutral and as irrelevant a question as, for instance, whether a certain enzyme in the liver of a chicken has mundane property A or mundane property B. When it comes to neutral and ultimately irrelevant questions like that, virtually no one has strong feelings one way or the other. Regardless of which fact turns out to be true upon closer analysis it will not have a significant impact on our lives, on our own worldview, or on our emotions. This is in stark contrast to the issue of whether an afterlife exists or not. Few questions are as important, relevant, or as close to the core of our entire worldview as the question of whether there exists an afterlife or not. Therefore, few people are able to evaluate the arguments and the data in favor of it or against it as dispassionately as the issue deserves, and are easily tempted into committing all kinds of subtle or even well-known fallacies. And this is true not only for those who are desperate to believe in the existence of an afterlife and who go on to do so for obviously bad reasons, such as the need for the feeling of existential comfort, but it is also true for those who prefer to think of themselves as rational, scientific, and skeptical disbelievers in the existence of an afterlife. When a person's core worldview is threatened, the defense mechanisms at their cognitive disposal go into overdrive and, consequently, all objectivity and logic tend to fly out of the window. A person finding themselves in such a situation will often grasp at whatever emotional straws, irrational rationalizations, or rhetorically disguised fallacies that they can and hold on to them for dear life in attempts to make the threatening information go away from their immediate awareness. Since the most intimate convictions and understandings about what reality is and how the world is structured is being challenged, it can often be a life-changing, arduous, and deeply uncomfortable experience for many people. Therefore, if you currently believe that there is not an afterlife, or that there probably is not an afterlife, or that we do not or can not know that there is an afterlife, and if this is an important conviction for you to hold on to, then this book might not turn out to be a pleasant read, since it will seriously challenge that conviction at its core root foundation. If you in the pursuit of truth, out of sheer curiosity, or for any other reason do go on to read this book despite holding any of these convictions and finding it important to hold on to these convictions, then I sincerely want to apologize in advance for the serious cognitive dissonance that you will very likely come to experience when embarking on the mental journey of new insights that this book will take you on.

Growing up as a rational person in Sweden, interested in science, philosophy, and the larger questions in life with justified answers to them, I unsurprisingly grew up as an atheist and as a materialist. Indeed, in general when a person grows up in Sweden, religion, spirituality, and what happens after death are largely irrelevant issues that are not considered so important that they are generally bothersome to most people. Back in 2006 when I was nineteen years old, however, I one day asked myself the following question: "Alright, whatever. What is the best argument in favor of the proposition that I am fundamentally wrong for having my current worldview?" After a lot of googling and reading around, I eventually found Neal Grossman's paper "Who's Afraid of Life After Death?", which explains why the evidence in favor of the existence of an afterlife is being systematically ignored, marginalized, and ridiculed not only by academia, but also by the religious institutions and, indeed, even by society at large. And while it did not go over the data in favor of the existence of an afterlife in great detail in and of itself, it did encourage me to start researching NDEs a lot more, and it eventually changed my entire perspective on everything when I discovered that there actually was solid empirical data to support what Neal Grossman had been arguing for in that paper.[1] I had not previously considered the possibility that the issue of whether an afterlife exists or not could be an empirical question. I thought it had just been, as he characterized it, a democratic issue where everyone is free to believe whatever he or she wants, but that we can not know anything about it through empirical investigation. What followed was years upon years of further research into the NDE and a lot of philosophical reflection and spiritual development on my own. I am now firmly convinced that an afterlife exists, and the argument that you are about to read is the main reason for that conviction as far as I have been able to articulate it. I can of course not predict whether it is as convincing to you as it is convincing to me, but this is still my best attempt at trying to put into words and materialize an argument that only has been hinted at before by some in the NDE research community.[2]

There are four well-established facts about the NDE that, on their own and from a purely scientific perspective, do not mean very much. But considered together and from a philosophical perspective, they form a tremendously compelling argument in favor of the existence of an afterlife. This is what NDE researcher Kenneth Ring had to say about two of these well-established facts about the NDE after having interviewed many near-death experiencers (NDErs) himself:

> [A]fter having spoken to many hundreds of NDErs, if not more than a thousand (for I have lost track by now), I have long become aware that from the **standpoint of NDErs themselves**, there is generally **no doubt** that the end of physical life is not a **dead** end. They confidently assert that there is something more. It has been my role and privilege often to speak for the many NDErs who do not write books or give public talks, and in doing so, I have often tried, as accurately as possible, to reflect the views of those NDErs whom I have chosen to represent. In doing so, I have tried to speak in their voice so that **they** would be heard, not me. In this respect, the evidence from NDEs is, I believe, highly suggestive that some form of consciousness continues after death; the abundant NDE testimony I have heard and read convinces me, as it does most others, of that.[3] (emphasis in original)

In other words, NDErs themselves are generally convinced, due to having had an NDE, that death is not the end that physicalism predicts, and very many people have had NDEs. These two facts, of course, prove nothing in and of themselves from a scientific point of view. Furthermore, the skeptic will rightfully point out that there are many other circumstances where very many people agree about something for bad reasons, and where we therefore can still not know whether what they assert is true or not from these two kinds of facts alone. Therefore, the next question we need to ask ourselves is whether NDErs have a good reason for being certain that death is not the end from having had an NDE. This is where the realer than real attribute of the NDE becomes highly relevant to investigate, and this is what Robert Perry has to say about that:

> There is clearly something about NDEs that both convinces people they are real and makes them distinguishable from experiences generally regarded as unreal. ... I've also heard NDErs say that their experiences were different from psychedelic drug experiences they had had.
>
> Actually, their claim often goes even further. Although in our eyes the question is whether NDEs are as real as this world, many NDErs say that what they experienced was **more** real than this world. ... What is it about NDEs that makes them seem to be more than dreams and hallucinations and to be even more real than the material world of everyday life? ... The question strikes me as extremely important. It seems to me that it has the potential to bridge some of that gulf between NDErs and the rest of us. They are overwhelmingly convinced that their experience was real. If we can gain some genuine understanding of why, then perhaps that will help us decide how much we can believe them.[4] (emphasis in original)

There is clearly something about the realer than real attribute of the phenomenology of the NDE that convinces NDErs themselves that the NDE is absolutely real in all interpretations of the term. That is, that the NDE was not just experienced as NDErs relay it, but that the NDE actually represented what it seemed to represent, that is, an experience of a higher reality than everyday life, and not a brain-generated hallucination. Of course, many skeptics of the survivalist interpretation of the NDE will often laughingly dismiss the realer than real attribute of the NDE and say that that proves nothing, as if contradicting a statement without providing any reason for doing so and accompanying such an action with laughter is a valid counterargument to anything. Or they will characterize NDEs as just very vivid dreams or hallucinations that therefore are as irrelevant as any other dream or hallucination, which just goes on to clearly demonstrate that they have neither carefully listened to nor charitably understood what NDErs are actually saying in the slightest. In the longest chapter of the book I go into great detail in breaking down the realer than real attribute of the NDE and demonstrate why it is the best possible justification of any empirical insight imaginable, and hence demonstrate why NDErs are absolutely epistemically justified in coming to the conclusion that the NDE represented what it seemed to represent.

So maybe the NDE convinces people for a good reason, the skeptic might concede, but how do we know that they are not biased? How do we know that they did not all believe in an afterlife prior to their NDE? Furthermore, how can we trust them? What if they are all lying, and just making it all up? How do we know that they evaluated the NDE and the realer than real attribute thereof skeptically and rationally? How do we know that they are not all crazy? This is where the fact that NDErs as a sample are representative of the population as a whole becomes highly relevant. As Neal Grossman points out:

> Research over the years has shown that there are no medical or psychological predictors of NDEs. ... What this means is that the sample of the population that reports NDEs is **representative** of the population as a whole. So if, say, 10% of the population are atheist-materialists, then about 10% of NDErs are, or were, atheist-materialists before their NDEs.[5] (emphasis in original)

Since NDErs as a sample are representative of the population as a whole, to disbelieve one hundred percent of NDErs is to disbelieve one hundred percent of the population. And to think that all NDErs are biased towards a survivalist interpretation, or that they are either untrustworthy, gullible, irrational, or delusional is to think that one hundred percent of the population also has at least one of those flaws. And how rational, reasonable, and realistic is that?

This is the core of the argument that will be presented in this book in much more detail, and it will be demonstrated how all of these facts considered together make it beyond astronomically likely and hence empirically certain that an afterlife exists. However, some people are definitely skeptical of the very idea that trying to establish anything as grandiose as the existence of an afterlife is possible, for the aforementioned reasoning that the issue is simply too controversial, important, and emotionally loaded to allow for objectivity in most people. NDE researcher Kenneth Ring articulated this skepticism very well when he wrote that:

> ... I am convinced that debates of this sort rarely settle anything. Disagreements between materialists and believers in some sort of transcendent reality have been raging since the days of Democritus and Plato and have never been resolved by either argument or evidence. And even since the beginnings of Spiritualism in the middle of the 19th century and extending through the subsequent rise of psychical research and finally into the modern era of near-death studies, nothing fundamentally has changed. Any reader familiar with the history and personages of the aforementioned domains will recognize that the contentions, **pro** and **con**, ... are merely replays of the same tedious speeches that have been declaimed throughout the years as believers and skeptics have faced off against each other.
>
> It is therefore both naïve and preposterous to think this comes down in the end to the matter of "evidence." It does not. People believe and will continue to believe what they do based on personal temperament, worldview, and the normative structure of their

reference groups. Thus, in my opinion, this exercise in opinion-mongering is a fruitless undertaking.[6] (emphasis in original)

While I recognize the merit in what he says to some degree, I still disagree with him that the situation is as hopeless as he tries to paint it as. Indeed, if I thoroughly agreed with him I would not have bothered to write this book in the first place. The situation, I will argue, is more nuanced than the idea that either everyone would follow the evidence or the arguments, or no one would. For instance, there are still people who seriously believe and maintain that the Earth is flat, despite mountains of evidence to the contrary. But does that mean that we can not come to the rational conclusion that there is sufficient evidence to make the case that the Earth is round? Of course not. Whether there is sufficient evidence for a proposition or not, or whether there are sufficiently cogent, compelling, and relevant arguments for a proposition or not is not a democratic issue where absolutely everyone has to agree or be persuaded before we can state as such. The fact that some people will never be persuaded by the evidence or by the arguments, come what may, does not mean that the evidence does not exist, or that the arguments are insufficiently cogent, compelling, or relevant from an objective viewpoint. And this does not change when we increase the number of people who refuse to follow the evidence or understand or engage with the arguments. If half of the world's population woke up tomorrow and insisted that the Earth was flat because of a bad reason, the Earth would still be round, and I would be just as persuaded by the evidence in favor of that proposition in that scenario as I am right now. Similarly, the fact that there are many millions of people who are currently materialists worldwide does not mean that there can not be valid evidence or rational arguments in favor of the existence of an afterlife. Their uninformed and metaphorical vote on the matter does not matter, the only matter that matters is whether the evidence or the arguments, or both, are sufficiently persuasive from an objective viewpoint to the individual thinker. So the fact that not everyone will even engage with the evidence or the arguments does not matter. And even when people do engage with the evidence or the arguments, many will not do so rationally or with an open mind and eager to find out about the actual truth. Many would rather do so with the intention to find a justification to continue believing what they currently do, however objectively invalid that perceived justification might be. This too, however, does not matter. The crucial point that I am trying to make, and where I disagree with Kenneth Ring and others who share his viewpoint, is that evidence or rational arguments, or both, can convince at least some people who have an open mind and who are genuinely interested in the actual truth of the matter, even though it will in all likelihood never get through to absolutely everyone.

It is therefore important to keep in mind that not all atheists, materialists, agnostics, or antitheists, etc., are all the same. Some of them are genuinely open-minded and inquisitive, but have not yet come across any arguments or any data that would make them rationally change their mind. I know that because I was once one of those people, and I did change my mind when I eventually came across arguments and data that were more persuasive than their denial. Indeed, since I am 33 years old at the time of this writing, and I grew up an atheist and a materialist, and I was 19 when I started to seriously research the NDE and changed my mind on the issue of whether an afterlife exists or not, I have technically still lived the majority of my life as far back as I can remember, albeit just barely, as an atheist and as a materialist who firmly and sincerely believed that this particular universe was in all probability all that existed. And I am certainly not alone, as I have been in countless discussions with people who have had a similar journey as me on this issue, and who started researching the NDE from the perspective that NDEs were probably hallucinations or illusions, but who were eventually persuaded or forced to change their minds when carefully and responsibly investigating the totality of the evidence and the arguments for and against that proposition.

But just like how some atheists, materialists, agnostics, or antitheists, etc., are genuinely open-minded and inquisitive, some are also definitely and demonstrably not. Philosopher of science Neal Grossman thoroughly recognized this long ago and was extremely serious when he coined the term fundamaterialism "to refer to those who believe that materialism is a necessary truth, not amenable to empirical evidence"[7] and "to characterize a person whose attitude towards materialism is the same as the fundamentalist's attitude towards his or her religion. In each case, the attitude is one of unwavering certainty towards the chosen ideology. For fundamaterialists, materialism does not appear to be an empirical hypothesis about the real world; it appears to be a given, an article of faith, the central tenet of his web of belief, around which everything else must conform."[8] For many otherwise intelligent and well-educated people, and especially for many in the upper echelons of academia, fundamaterialism is so deeply ingrained into the core of their minds that they can no longer see alternatives to materialism as serious possibilities, and are vehemently resistant to the idea that materialism can be falsified by empirical data. Indeed, they are especially vehemently against the idea that it already has been falsified by empirical data. Whether genuinely meant or not, they will often say things like, "Yeah, it may be falsified one day in the future, but it has not yet been falsified," all the while they have overwhelmingly often not actually examined all of the proposed evidence in favor of the proposition that they are denying. This is known as perpetually moving the goalposts into the future and delaying the day of reckoning indefinitely, a well-known informal fallacy that will always be near at hand and tempting for the rhetorically gifted fundamaterialist. And the absurdity of the situation is of course compounded by the fact that they commit such a well-known informal fallacy and say such things about a vast body of evidence and arguments that they are not actually intimately familiar with and have not carefully and responsibly investigated.

While this book is admittedly about a philosophical argument in favor of the existence of an afterlife rather than primarily being about scientific data, the philosophical argument is based on four non-controversial empirical facts about the NDE. And the argument is not merely that it might become obvious that there is an afterlife in the future, but that it is obvious right now that there is an afterlife in light of these four empirical facts. This is why I am trying to explain and illustrate how some people are known to be deeply resistant on a psychological level against that idea, regardless of whether they are sufficiently capable, self-aware, or willing to acknowledge it or not, whether publicly or even to themselves. And indeed, the sociological roots of fundamaterialism should not be underestimated or ignored, as there is a tremendous peer pressure within the current academic climate to be a fundamaterialist. Of course, when it comes to the vast majority of subjects that can be studied at university level, it is simply not relevant whether the afterlife exists or not, or whether materialism is true or not. But in the subjects where it is extremely relevant, such as in psychology and especially in philosophy, the issue of NDEs and similar phenomena are rarely even brought up at all, and if they are they are just ridiculed, marginalized, or ignored, rather than taken as seriously as they should be. As Neal Grossman notes:

It would seem that, of all the disciplines, philosophy ought to be most interested in, and meticulously study, all the research on the NDE. After all, is philosophy not supposed to be concerned with questions of ultimate meaning, of the purpose of life, of the relation between mind and body, of God, and so on? NDE research has *data that are directly relevant to all of these questions. So how is it possible that philosophers have collectively managed to ignore and even ridicule this research? To those outside of academic philosophy, it may come as a surprise to learn the great majority of academic philosophers are atheists and materialists. While ... they incorrectly use science to support their materialism, they systematically ignore the findings of science — which I take near-death research to be — that refute their materialism. Since their materialism is not empirically based, I call it fundamaterialism, to make explicit comparison with fundamentalism in religion. Fundamentalism connotes an attitude of certainty towards one's core belief. Just as the fundamentalist Christian is absolutely certain that the world was created in the manner described by the Bible — fossil evidence notwithstanding — so also the fundamaterialist is absolutely certain that there exists nothing that is not made up of matter — NDEs and other evidence notwithstanding. In fact, and this is the crucial point, their respective beliefs have nothing to do with evidence. As my fundamaterialist colleague put it: "There can't be evidence for something that's false." ... [F]undamaterialist philosophers believe in the truth of materialism **a priori**; empirical evidence is not relevant to them, and they are committed to ignoring and/or debunking anything that looks like evidence.*[9] (emphasis in original)

Unbeknownst to many people in the general population, and contrary to what one might hope for from the presumed ideal of a thinker, many if not most philosophers are actually strikingly dogmatic about the worldview and general set of beliefs that they developed and internalized during their formative years. Furthermore, many if not most philosophers also have so much invested in their current worldview that they often in practice see it as a career necessity not to change their minds, or they simply feel that they do not have the time or the energy to change their worldview and reset their understanding of reality. Indeed, this is so common that it essentially becomes major headlines in the philosophy world when a well-known philosopher actually does change his or her mind in the middle of or at the end of their career (e.g., Wittgenstein). Few things about the current state of philosophy are as dispiriting as this, because being wrong and admitting as such not only to yourself but also to the entire world is something that should be enthusiastically celebrated, and not made fun of, looked down upon, or be seen as an admission of failure. Indeed, there is no greater sign of intellectual integrity, courage, and virtue than when a person admits both to themselves and to everyone else that they have been wrong about something, and the closer to the core of their entire worldview that that thing is then the much more impressive it is, because the much harder it was to do. And I do not at all care if someone changes their mind from believing what I currently do about something to its exact opposite, because I would still like to genuinely throw them a party and shower them with admiration and support for having that much intellectual integrity, courage, and virtue. When a person admits to themselves and everyone else that they were wrong before, they are updating their understanding of things when new information or new insights become available. Would it not be wonderful if all or at least most philosophers could just drop their stubborn and meaningless sense of intellectual pride in persisting in believing what they have always believed, as if they are the ultimate philosopher of all time who realized all core truths for all time to come when they were young, or if they could drop their fear of seeing things in an entirely new light later on in life, or if they could drop their fear of what all of their peers and colleagues will think of such a course of action? If they could and would do this, philosophy as an enterprise could and would move on much faster than it currently does, instead of mirroring the quip that science abides by in that science advances one funeral at a time. Right now, in practice, philosophy also advances one funeral at a time. We can only really hope that the philosophy world addresses the fact that the history of philosophy and the contemporary state thereof is a quagmire of ideological stubbornness and individual dogma more seriously at some point, and put much more emphasis on encouraging the next generations of philosophers to be acutely aware of it from the very start so that they do not have their own set of core beliefs set in stone.

And sadly, that many aspiring and budding philosophers, who might otherwise be more open-minded than their professors, are still reluctant to take the NDE seriously probably has to some degree to do with the fact that it is not currently seen as a serious alternative for those who wish to pursue a career in academic philosophy and eventually get tenure to do so. In other words, they will have to hide or downplay their interest in NDEs while still on the track to getting tenure and relative financial security, since, for instance, publishing articles that are friendly to the survivalist interpretation of NDEs in the most prestigious philosophy journals is currently next to impossible. And this is the case not because the quality of the data or the arguments are subpar, but rather because of how controversial and taboo the nature of the subject itself currently is to many if not most academic philosophers. Therefore, if or when the survivalist interpretation of NDEs becomes recognized by the profession as the respectable majority stance in the future, then at least this and the end of the last century will probably be seen as very embarrassing episodes in the history of philosophy when, at the very least, there was a serious failure of curiosity and courage of monumental proportions to investigate the NDE more enthusiastically, objectively, fairly, and extensively. At least right now it can be said, metaphorically speaking, that the academic philosophy world is sleeping so soundly, peacefully, and innocently in the starfish position on the topic of NDEs that you can practically hear the collective snoring even from outer space.

But it is not just fundamaterialists and set in their cognitive ways philosophers and scientists who have irrational problems with arguments or evidence, or both, in favor of the existence of an afterlife. There are also those who seem to be operating from the rigid cognitive framework not necessarily that materialism must be true, but rather from some kind of agnostic dogma in that they are unwaveringly convinced that neither we nor anyone else can ever know what happens when we die or that an afterlife exists. But for what non-dogmatic reason do they justifiably know that it is demonstrably, necessarily, and eternally true that neither we nor anyone else can ever justifiably know the answers to such questions? From what insight are they so unwaveringly convinced that neither direct experience, scientific data, nor philosophical arguments can ever satisfactorily and justifiably answer such questions? Some people sometimes say things along the lines of, "Nobody knows or can know what happens when we die," or, "Nobody knows or can know that an afterlife exists." And of course they follow it up with saying something like, "And if anyone says that they do have the answers to these questions, then they simply must be lying or mistaken." But how do they, in turn, know that? How do they actually know that neither themselves nor others can know what happens when we die, or that neither themselves nor others can know that an afterlife exists? It seems to me, as I wrote earlier, to just be a reflection of an unexamined agnostic dogma.

Furthermore, after having been in discussions about the issue of the existence of an afterlife my entire adult life, I have seen numerous times how some people, after being figuratively cornered by arguments and evidence, have simply stated that they will not believe in the reality of an afterlife, no matter what, since their own minds simply will not let them. They have said that they can not do so, even if they should be forced to do so by rational arguments and empirical evidence, because their feelings of incredulity are simply too strong. This is of course self-evidently fallacious reasoning, but many people still use it as an argument in their own minds to rationalize these feelings of incredulity. What they think is something along the lines of, "I can not actually believe it because my feelings of incredulity are too strong, therefore the data is not good enough, or the arguments are not sufficiently cogent, compelling, or relevant." What they should think if they were self-aware and honest with themselves is instead, "I can not actually believe it because my feelings of incredulity are too strong, therefore my feelings cloud my judgment. I should instead ask myself whether the empirical evidence is good enough from an objective viewpoint, or whether the rational arguments are cogent, compelling, and relevant from an objective viewpoint, regardless of whether the evidence or the arguments, or both, are capable of overriding my extremely powerful but ultimately irrational and irrelevant feelings of incredulity." The fact that we can not actually believe in something in our own mind is irrelevant to whether something is actually true or real. So I can only feel genuine sympathy for those who can not believe in an afterlife, no matter what. Their minds have them in a perpetual prison of disbelief on important issues like this, and which for these reasons makes it harder for them than for the rest of us to evaluate the arguments and the data dispassionately and much more objectively. But the question those who suffer from this perpetual state of incredulity should ask themselves is not whether the arguments and the data have been able to override their extremely strong feelings of incredulity, but whether the data is good enough from an objective viewpoint, or whether the arguments are sufficiently cogent, compelling, and relevant from an objective viewpoint. If they find that this is the case, they should realize that they should therefore objectively infer the conclusion that an afterlife exists, regardless of how they feel about its existence, and regardless of whether they can actually believe in its existence in their own minds.

So there are the fundamaterialists who think that there simply can be no empirical data that should warrant us to infer the existence of an afterlife, and there are those who are a bit more open-minded about it, but who are still stuck in a perpetual state of disbelief on the issue because their feelings of incredulity are simply too strong. The former group of people are clearly not reachable with the argument that is being presented in this book, just like religious fundamentalists can not be reached with empirical data that clearly demonstrate the past existence of dinosaurs. But the latter group of people might be – but only if they are diligently aware of what was just written in the former paragraph and evaluate the argument from that perspective. Since we know that fundamentalists and fundamaterialists exist, we do know that some people just want to either believe or disbelieve in an afterlife no matter what, and they will continue to do so regardless of what has been written, explained, and argued for in this book, or regardless of what has been written, explained, and argued for in any other book either for that matter. So this book is clearly not written for those whose minds emulate the ostrich on ideologically sensitive subjects like this, for trying to write such a book would be the very definition of futility. Instead, it has been written for those who are genuinely interested in and open-minded about whether there exists an afterlife or not, regardless of whether they currently think so, or whether they are sitting on the metaphorical fence on this issue and have a hard time figuring out what to think, or whether they currently do not think so. Open-minded and inquisitive people on the issue of whether an afterlife exists or not will enjoy reading this book and contemplating and exploring the argument even further. Indeed, since all knowledge and all discussions are ultimately fractal in nature, it is impossible for me to respond to and exhaust all possible counterarguments and their minutiae in advance. I can only refute and highlight the most common and predictable counterarguments and fallacies, and this argument, like virtually all other philosophical arguments, will ultimately go on long after the death of the author. Any argument for anything in philosophy (besides those in pure logic) is ultimately, in practice, just a conversation starter, and it is up to history and everyone else to determine for themselves and amongst each other whether the argument is ultimately cogent, compelling, and relevant. And if the reader can find a flaw in the argument, or find ways to improve it, I highly encourage the reader to do so and reflect even further and in more depth on the argument. So this book should by no means be thought of as the final word on this argument, but hopefully rather as just the solid beginning of a long-lasting conversation.

Chapter 2

The Four Premises

An NDE can be broadly defined as an unusual and lucid experience that occurs at a time of an imminent life-threatening event. Research has shown that they occur in roughly 9-18% of all cardiac arrests, with no sufficient nor necessary cause having been identified for why they happen to some and not to all, making every one of us a potential NDEr were we to come close to death ourselves.[10] NDEs often include perceptions of leaving the body, feeling peaceful, entering a tunnel or passageway, seeing or even entering a light, meeting deceased relatives, meeting a being of light, going through a life review, experiencing an overwhelming sense of unconditional love and acceptance, etc. While no two NDEs are the same and can have any possible combination of elements, they have almost always some of these types of core elements to them, and the more of them that is experienced by a single individual the deeper the NDE is defined to be by the researchers in the field, being categorizable as subtle, deep, and profound NDEs accordingly.[11]

In this book it is argued that it is beyond astronomically likely and hence empirically certain that an afterlife exists in light of the following four non-controversial facts about the NDE:

1. The overwhelming majority of people who have an NDE become personally convinced of the reality of survival and an afterlife based on their experience, and the prevalence of this aftereffect is strongly correlated with the depth of the NDE.[12]
2. An NDEr will more often than not say that the reality they encountered while they were going through this experience was a lot more real than this reality we participate in as

humans on a daily basis, and the prevalence of this attribute is strongly correlated with the depth of the NDE.[13]

3. More than forty years of scholarly research has shown that no physiological, psychological, nor sociological predictor has yet been identified as either necessary or sufficient to cause or prohibit an NDE or its depth when someone has a survived proximity to death. Therefore, NDEs are equal opportunity experiences and NDErs as a sample are representative of the population as a whole. The percentage of subtle, deep, and profound NDErs who were uncertain about or skeptical of the existence of an afterlife prior to their NDE is therefore roughly the same as the percentage of people who are uncertain about or skeptical of the existence of an afterlife in the population as a whole. Similarly, the percentage of subtle, deep, and profound NDErs who are generally trustworthy, skeptical, rational, and sane is roughly the same as the percentage of people who are generally trustworthy, skeptical, rational, and sane in the population as a whole.[14]

4. Millions of people, probably even tens of millions of people, have had NDEs.[15]

This argument will be made by creating a thought experiment that demonstrates and emphasizes the epistemic relevance of converging and justified testimonies by randomly selected people in large numbers, and then by elaborating on the epistemic, metaphysical, and phenomenological relevance of the realer than real attribute of the NDE. For simplicity of presentation, let us intentionally overgeneralize and assume for the next two chapters that the first and second facts were such that all NDErs became convinced of the existence of an afterlife, and that all NDErs felt that the NDE was a lot more real than this life. The significance of how the data falls short of this scenario will be analyzed in the fifth chapter.

Chapter 3

The Room

Imagine that some very rich people built a very specific room. This room was designed and constructed in such a way that there was no way whatsoever of learning anything about what was inside of it from studying it on the outside. No X-ray, no heat camera, no radar, no satellite, no micro aerial vehicle, no instrument of any kind could detect anything about what was inside of this room. The people who designed and built the room were acutely aware of all the world-leading research in the fields of all the technologies that might aid in learning anything about what is on its inside from the outside, and designed the room in such a way as to completely neutralize all such attempts. Furthermore, the room was kept in a high-security building with cameras and excessive security protocols and technologies everywhere. Simply put, no one who was unauthorized to go into the room could ever access it.

However, the very rich people who built the room did let people into the room occasionally, selecting them completely at random. As a result, most people who were randomly selected to go in there usually only did so once in their lifetime and only for a limited amount of time. Their visit to the room, however, was of sufficient duration to give them a fair chance to thoroughly investigate whatever they would find inside of the room.

When they were selected to go into the room, they could not bring with them anything that could communicate with the outside world. That is, no Internet devices, no mobile phones, etc., and it would be carefully checked that no such device came with them. Once in the room, however, the randomly selected people could explore it as carefully as they wished. They could touch, smell, see, hear, and taste everything that was in it, and they could use whatever devices they brought with them to verify the reality of whatever they happened to find in the room.

When they left the room, however, they would go through a meticulous screening process once again which made sure that nothing in the room was left on or in them and that there was no physical evidence of what was inside the room that they could take with them. Whatever devices or tools they brought into the room to verify the reality of whatever they came to find in there were confiscated upon leaving it, and these devices or tools were subsequently either destroyed or thoroughly neutralized, such that if they were recycled there would be no clues whatsoever on them or in them of what the randomly selected people going into the room had found in there. When the randomly selected people got out of the room, the only evidence of what was inside of the room that they could bring with them and share with the rest of the world was their own testimony of what they experienced in there.

Here is where the interesting questions arise. After how many randomly selected people going through this process, and everyone reporting essentially the same thing about what they found in there, is it reasonable to start believing in them and infer knowledge from their cumulative and converging testimonies? And to what degree is the extraordinary nature of the claim of what is in there relevant to this number?

While it is not in dispute that testimonies do transmit knowledge, it must also be noted that testimonies have certain shortcomings compared to other ways of gathering knowledge.[16] For instance, memory and perception in human beings is faulty, people can lie and many people do lie about various issues with varying degrees of frequency for various reasons, and some people are easily fooled by misleading appearances (such as optical illusions). Additionally, as the magnitude of converging testimonies increases, there always remains the logical possibility that everyone is participating in some kind of conspiracy of global proportions. These and similar considerations certainly lessen the epistemic impact of any given testimony. However, for every increase in magnitude of the amount of randomly selected people who enter the room, these and similar objections carry less and less weight, as the probabilistic argument that such considerations can account for the observations loses strength as the number of observations increases.

If one randomly selected person goes into the room and reports that there is a brown table with a white plate on it, it might be indicative to some degree of what is in there. However, the person could certainly be lying, or be seriously incapable of telling the mere appearance of a brown table with a white plate on it apart from its actual existence, or they might just be careless in their investigation thereof. Taking one single testimony by a single randomly selected person as good evidence of what is really in there might therefore be unwarranted. This is because it is not entirely unlikely that that randomly selected person is among the percentage of the population that are either untrustworthy or unqualified epistemic agents, that is, people who are either unable or uneager to do a proper job of thoroughly investigating whatever is in there. However, if ten randomly selected people go into the room and report that there is a brown table with a white plate on it and nothing more, it may be reasonable to start believing them at once. This is because it is a lot less likely that they would all be lying about the same thing, especially since they have no connection to each other, and since it is a lot less likely that they would all be untrustworthy or unqualified epistemic agents. After one hundred randomly selected people reporting that there really is a brown table with a white plate on it in that room, few people among the rest of us would likely still remain skeptical about what they reported. After one thousand randomly selected people going in and all reporting that there really is a brown table with a white plate on it in that room, would there still be a single skeptic? If so, how would they justify that skepticism?

Of course, it is possible in the philosophical interpretation of the term that one thousand randomly selected people are all lying, mistaken, or misled by their experience of that room, and no amount of randomly selected people all reporting to have observed the same thing in that room will ever prove it to be factual with one hundred percent infallible certainty. But how likely is it to be the case in reality that one thousand converging and justified testimonies by randomly selected people are all mistaken? Philosophers love to entertain the most outlandish and beyond astronomically unlikely possibilities, but it is important to keep in mind that that is precisely what such skepticism represents in such a case, and is not a reasonable and realistic interpretation of the situation.

This is an extremely important point that can not be emphasized enough. The subtle fallacy of appealing to what is logically possible but also empirically extremely unlikely, as if doing so is somehow a relevant counterargument to anything, tends to be committed again and again in discussions about ideologically sensitive empirical matters. Therefore it is important to preempt the allure of this way of thinking right from the start, and make clear that there is a tremendous difference between a logical possibility and an empirical possibility. A logical possibility is anything that can be consistently stated without self-contradiction, however unlikely it may be that it is true in the real world. An empirical possibility, on the other hand, is something that is reasonably likely to be true in the real world and has at least some degree of evidential support. All empirical possibilities also have to be logical possibilities, but the reverse is not true. An example of a logical possibility is that there could be an advanced alien civilization living under the surface of the planet Mars right now, whereas an example of an empirical possibility is when the weatherman says that it could rain tomorrow. The former example does not violate the laws of logic, but there is absolutely no empirical evidence to suggest that it might be true or even remotely likely and that we should therefore take it seriously. The second example usually has some degree of evidential support, so that it is not wildly unlikely that the weatherman could be correct. For any given explanation of anything in an empirical context, there is always a practically infinite list of logically possible alternative explanations that also could, in theory, explain it. For instance, it is logically possible that the sun is actually a spaceship that is merely disguising itself as a star. But is it therefore reasonable to not conclude that the sun is a star, just because of such an ever-present logical possibility to the contrary? Clearly not. Being empirical is all about making unbiased inferences to the most likely explanation. So unless there are empirical reasons to think that any one of such alternative explanations are actually likely to some relevant degree and are hence empirical possibilities, there is no reason to entertain any one of them seriously in an empirical context.[17]

Clearly no or very few people are absolutely honest about all things at all times, and clearly no or very few people lie about absolutely everything all the time. Clearly no or very few people are skeptical about every single detail of what they experience and of what they are told about all the time, and clearly no or very few people gullibly believe in everything as it first appears or in absolutely everything that they are told about. Clearly no or very few people are as rational as humanly possible, and clearly no or very few people are as irrational as humanly possible. Clearly no or very few people are as sane as humanly possible, and clearly no or very few people are as delusional as humanly possible. These human character traits find themselves on a spectrum between two extremes, and all human beings have each of them to varying degrees. So when it is said that a person is trustworthy, skeptical, rational, and sane, then that simply means that they are sufficiently trustworthy, skeptical, rational, and sane so that they can generally be safely regarded as such, even if they do not have each of these character traits maxed out to absolute perfection. Likewise, when it is said that someone is either untrustworthy, gullible, irrational, or delusional, then that means that they have at least one of these character traits to a sufficient degree where they can generally be safely regarded as having such a character trait.

Obviously the percentage of the population that are demonstrably untrustworthy, gullible, irrational, or delusional is not zero, as virtually everyone would agree without much objection that at least some people have at least one of those character traits to a significantly alarming degree. Furthermore, children are in general less skeptical and less rational than adults are, and the younger they are the less capable they are in general of doing a thorough investigation of whether what appears to be inside of the room really is there. And since infants are a part of the population but can neither communicate nor access explicit recall of their memories, their presence in the room would be irrelevant. And while that is definitely the case for infants entering the room, it is arguably not the case for infant NDErs, as they can actually remember their NDE and can inform others about it when they eventually learn to talk.[18] Either way, there is no real discussion worth to be had about the fact that at least a certain percentage of the population are either untrustworthy or incapable of telling the mere appearance of something apart from its actual existence.

However, while some might want to entertain the extreme notion that zero percent of the population can be trusted and regarded as capable of investigating what is inside of that room, it is important to understand that if this was true, it would make an epistemic civilization impossible. This is because everyone would have to start from absolute scratch themselves when learning anything at all about the world, and that is clearly not the world we live in. Even our most respectable sources of objective empirical knowledge depend on the sort of testimonies that can be gained about what is inside of this room, since scientific studies are ultimately just a few testimonies in written form that are being peer reviewed, which really just adds a few more testimonies as justification for the confidence we can have in the reported data. The scientists presumably do the work, report in written form about what they did, how they did it, and what they found, and the peer reviewers report to the editor or the editorial team that they confirmed the validity of the studies. But objectively and ultimately, what is happening is that a few testimonies, both by the scientists and the peer reviewers, are being put forth as claims of knowledge by presumably trustworthy and qualified epistemic agents. Even if other scientists duplicate the studies, or double-check them, this ultimately just adds more testimonies as justification for the confidence we can have in the reported data. Therefore, all of our best objective empirical knowledge about the world ultimately relies on the validity of testimonies as conveyors thereof, and on the crucial fact that at least a certain percentage of the population can be regarded as trustworthy and qualified epistemic agents.[19]

So we do know that neither all nor none of the population can be regarded as trustworthy and qualified epistemic agents. And clearly we do not know exactly what the percentage of the population is that can be regarded as trustworthy, skeptical, rational, and sane, and it is highly doubtful whether we will ever know it with absolute precision, especially given the fact that new people are born, raised differently, and die all the time. We can only ever argue for reasonable estimations based on a multitude of considerations. But it will not here be argued for any such reasonable estimation. Instead, it will just be demonstrated that, even if we are deeply paranoid or cynical about the trustworthiness and capability of our fellow human beings and assume the worst case scenario (within reason), it is still beyond astronomically unlikely that all randomly selected people would be convincingly lying or mistaken about what would be inside of the room as soon as a lot of them have had the chance to enter and investigate it.

If the very rich people were to open up this room for all to investigate after one thousand randomly selected people going through this process, should we all expect to find anything other than what the one thousand and first randomly selected person entering the room should also expect to find? And how often should we expect to find anything other than what the one thousand randomly selected people had already reported to be in there, if ever? It seems at least intuitively to be the case that if they were ever to be wrong, it would be a beyond astronomically rare event. Should we expect it to happen even once if this experiment was to be repeated a thousand times with reports of different mundane objects inside each time the experiment was repeated? What about if we repeated it a million, or even a billion times? Indeed, if this experiment was repeated a billion times and one thousand randomly selected people got it exactly right each and every time, how could someone seriously try to maintain that testimonies do not transmit knowledge, or that they do not transmit the justification of knowledge, and that it must therefore just be a purely irrelevant coincidence that they got it exactly right each and every time? Indeed, if testimonies transmitted neither knowledge nor its justification, then it would be extremely unlikely that they would get it exactly right even once. This is because even if we only consider mundane things as possibilities of what could be inside of the room, there are still immeasurably more than a billion different things or variations of things that could be there instead of what everyone reported. And what about if we repeated the experiment 10^{50}, a googol, or even 10^{200} times? While these are unfathomably large numbers that could not feasibly be carried out in practice, it still seems intuitively unlikely that one thousand randomly selected people would all be convincingly lying about the same thing or be wrong about what would be in there even once.

Still, let us for the sake of argument assume that fifty percent of the population are either untrustworthy or incapable of telling the difference between the mere appearance of something from its actual existence when given the chance to investigate it thoroughly, for whatever reason. If fifty percent of the population are not qualified to investigate the matter and have a relevant and trustworthy judgment, and if people are selected at random to go into the room, then it essentially becomes a coin flip whether anyone going in there is trustworthy and capable of investigating the matter. The probability that all one thousand randomly selected people going into the room are thus either untrustworthy or incapable of investigating whether the object is actually there or merely an illusion is 0.5^{1000}, or roughly 9.3×10^{-302}. Even if we raise the percentage of people we either can not trust or who are incapable of investigating the matter from fifty percent to ninety percent of the population, the probability that all one thousand people who are randomly selected to go in there belong to this cohort is still 0.9^{1000}, or roughly 1.7×10^{-46}. If we go from ninety percent to ninety-nine percent of the population, the probability that no trustworthy and qualified epistemic agent enters the room becomes 0.99^{1000}, or roughly 0.00004317. If we keep the assumption that ninety-nine percent of the population are either untrustworthy or incapable of investigating that room in a scrutinous manner, and raise the amount of randomly selected people who enter the room by one magnitude to ten thousand instead of one thousand, then the probability that no trustworthy and qualified epistemic agent gets to enter that room jumps back down to the astronomical improbability of 0.99^{10000}, or roughly 2.2×10^{-44}. Can these or similar assumptions, scenarios, or possibilities therefore be considered relevant counterarguments to the claim that it is extremely likely that what one thousand randomly selected people or more report to be in the room is really there?

Of course, at first reflection it is not entirely unthinkable that the very rich people would or could have placed a team of professional persuaders in the room that would bribe, threaten, or bribe and threaten the randomly selected people who entered the room in order to make the randomly selected people tell a specific lie about what was in the room once they exited the room. But again, that just boomerangs back to the issue of trustworthiness and the general implausibility and improbability of creating and maintaining global conspiracies with lots of people involved. Additionally, it is not just a matter of what all people would do in such a situation and when faced with such a choice, but also of what they could do. Would and could one hundred percent of the population tell a convincing lie, both immediately and in the long run? Would and could they all conceal their newfound wealth for the rest of their lives to not raise suspicions to any outsiders, and would all find it worth it if they had to live that way? Would and could they all conceal the trauma of being threatened, both immediately and in the long run? While many people would probably gladly tell a trivial lie to the rest of the world for all time to come for some money, it is easy to see how far from all would. For instance, some people are either already rich, or for other reasons do not really care about acquiring (more) money. Other people are either seriously suicidal or imminently dying anyway and have no friends or family to care about, and can be neither bribed nor threatened with anything worldly. Some people hate rich people, capitalism, the monetary system, or the idea of being manipulated or bought by those in power. Some people would love to be the whistle-blower to a conspiracy. Some people love the truth more than anything else. Some people simply do not want to live with the constant pressure of having to maintain a lie. Some people would reason that the truth would probably come out quickly anyway, and would not want their reputation tarnished. And so on. Indeed, there are probably far more reasons for why some people would not want to accept a lifelong commitment for a bribe that also has to be kept hidden and secret anyway than I can enumerate here, or for that matter even imagine.

Furthermore, it is also easy to see how far from all people could convincingly tell a trivial lie to the rest of the world for all time to come. For instance, some people with various developmental disorders such as certain manifestations of high-functioning autism or Asperger syndrome tell the blunt, brutal, upsetting, and unvarnished truth basically all the time no matter what. But many people also reliably give off obvious clues when they are lying. These are usually unusual shifts in body movements, facial expressions, tone of voice, or the content of their speech. Of course, just like many people are bad at lying, so too are many people bad at detecting lies. Some randomly selected people coming out of the room who are skilled at lying would therefore definitely be able to convincingly lie to some people on the outside of the room about what was in there, at least on some occasions. But the crucial point is that we have no reason to think that all of the randomly selected people coming out of the room would be able to convincingly lie to everyone on the outside of that room for all time to come about what was in there, and especially not to those who are trained experts in detecting when someone is likely lying. Furthermore, is it really reasonable to assume that one hundred percent of the population would never confide to their friends or family members about the actual truth, or never cave in when pressed about the issue, or never let the truth slip out by mistake at some point, such as when or if they are drunk or on·drugs? Of course, some might argue against the room analogy by making the point that the randomly selected people entering the room are not just bribed, threatened, or bribed and threatened in the room to make them tell a specific lie, but are also given a world-class crash course in how to convincingly lie. But can one hundred percent of the population really learn how to become good liars in such a short time period? And even if they could, that would be a noticeable aftereffect that would show up in their life in general after they exited the room. Indeed, if everyone came out of the room as suddenly a skilled liar, that would raise serious suspicions in its own right. Of course, it could be argued that they became such good liars that they just used their skills only when talking about what was inside of the room, and then faked ineptitude at lying for the rest of their lives in all other situations to not raise suspicions, and acted as if they were roughly as bad liars as before. But given how difficult it is for many of us to learn things fast, well, and in a way that it sticks for life even when we go to school, it is really hard to imagine how the people in the room could realistically implant such lifelong discipline and skills in one hundred percent of the population with so little time to work with.

Some people have a natural inclination for lying whenever they judge that it benefits them, but some definitely do not. Similarly, some people have a natural talent for lying convincingly and for their entire lives about something, but some definitely do not. For instance, while even young children in the ages three to eight years old can attempt to tell lies, they are also demonstrably less good at it than older children, teenagers, and adults.[20] And since people in this age bracket are at least roughly five percent of the population (but probably more), it would quickly become very unlikely as hundreds of randomly selected people and beyond had entered the room that none of them would be a part of this cohort. So no matter how cynical (within reason) we are about people's trustworthiness, or how optimistic (within reason) we are about their ability to convincingly lie not just immediately but also for the rest of their lives, the probability that all randomly selected people who entered the room would and could be telling a convincing lie would still drop precipitously long before we reached one thousand randomly selected people entering the room.

Furthermore, if the bribe did not come attached with any threat as a disincentive against accepting the money and telling the truth anyway, then is it not very likely that at least some people would accept the money and then tell the truth anyway? And while many people would probably judge that it would be worth it to tell a trivial lie to avoid the realization of a threat, far from all people would accept being threatened and having to live with it, and would just go to the police or talk about it on social media immediately instead to bring worldwide attention to the issue, which would in turn probably encourage more people who had gone into the room to come forward about what really happened and existed in there. Furthermore, some people would very likely be so upset from the trauma of being threatened that it would be evident when they exited the room and were interviewed that something really bad happened in there and that they were in all probability not telling the truth. And while some scientists sometimes fabricate, falsify, or modify data or results for a variety of reasons, including for perceived benefits to themselves personally,[21] science as an epistemic enterprise would be useless and irrelevant if we did not trust scientists in general anyway. That some very rich people are ultimately bribing, threatening, or bribing and threatening all scientists and the editorial teams of all scientific journals to make the public believe certain false things about the world is and will of course always remain logically possible. However, to be so extremely and unduly cynical and paranoid about the world, society, and human nature as to therefore disregard the global scientific enterprise as a valid, relevant, and trustworthy epistemic source is hardly the most rational course of action.

Of course, well worth mentioning is also that there are some people in the population who are either highly delusional or compulsive liars. So no matter what actually is in the room, whether it is nothing, some mundane object or objects, some people who are trying to bribe, threaten, or bribe and threaten the people who enter, or something seemingly extraordinary, or whatever else, we should still expect at least some testimonies to occasionally be divergent or in disagreement with the general consensus. However, what is crucial is to determine what kind of people are supplying the testimonies that are divergent and in disagreement, and why they do so. If we find that these testimonies are by people who are highly delusional or compulsive liars in the context of their daily life outside of the room, then these testimonies can be safely considered expected and are thus largely irrelevant. It is only when the testimonies which are divergent and in disagreement with the general consensus are by people who are the most trustworthy, skeptical, rational, and sane in the context of their daily life outside of the room that we should start to worry.

At least when it comes to mundane claims of what is inside of that room, whatever is reported to justifiably exist in the room is clearly extremely likely to be true when it is extremely likely that many trustworthy and qualified epistemic agents have investigated that room and have all come to the same justified conclusion. The next interesting question worth investigating is therefore what happens when we increase the extraordinary nature of what is being reported to exist in that room. While it may intuitively seem to be the case for some or even many of us at first, does the epistemic situation actually change at all? And if so, how and why? The epistemic situation does not actually change just because of our enhanced feelings of incredulity from hearing about whatever the randomly selected people may report to exist or transpire in there. Nor does the epistemic situation change because of our current worldview disallowing for what the randomly selected people report to justifiably exist or transpire in there. Nor does the epistemic situation change because of how familiar we may be or not be with the content, material, structure, behavior, or concept of the things or events that are reported to exist or transpire in the room. And nor does the epistemic situation change because of how bad our limited imagination may be at imagining what it would be like to experience the extraordinary things or events in the room. However strong our skepticism or our skeptical reaction may be to hearing what everyone reports to exist or transpire in that room, and for whatever reason we hold on to that skepticism, we can be comfortably certain of the fact that a significant percentage of the randomly selected people going into the room shared our skepticism and the justification for our skepticism before going into the room themselves. Indeed, to any outsiders besides ourselves we are just another potentially randomly selected person going into the room, and they would, from their perspective, have no reason at all to think that our skeptical feelings and the justification we have for those feelings would yield a different outcome when investigating the room than it would for everyone else going in there. Therefore, our incredulity, or our worldview-preserving defense mechanisms generating an emotional reluctance to accept what everyone reports to exist or transpire in there, or our lack of familiarity with what everyone reports to exist or transpire in there, or how bad we may be at imagining what it is like to experience the extraordinary thing or event in there are all considerations that are rationally and objectively irrelevant to whether the thing that they report to be in there really is in there or not.

Of course, a common objection that has often been raised when it comes to the potential validity of extraordinary sounding claims is that extraordinary claims require extraordinary evidence.[22] However, this aphorism has historically just been used as an unexamined catchphrase to prematurely and irrationally dismiss unorthodox ideas out of hand, instead of following the evidence no matter where it leads regardless of how we feel about or subjectively judge the claims. In other words, if we want to be objective in a scholarly context we always have to follow the totality of the evidence, no matter where it leads. Our personal and subjective feelings of amazement towards certain claims do not mean that we can suddenly demand an arbitrary, undefined, and perpetually increasing amount of more evidence for those claims, for then we have already conceded the claim to objectivity and neutrality. So if a given quality and quantity of evidence in favor of a claim we do not deem amazing should make us infer that the claim is true, then the same quality and quantity of evidence in favor of a claim we do deem amazing should also be equally convincing and sufficient. Claims that we deem to be extraordinary do not require evidence that we deem to be extraordinary, they just demand the same quality and quantity of evidence that claims that we deem to be ordinary do. Or to put it simply, extraordinary sounding claims do not require extraordinary sounding evidence, they just require evidence.[23] Of course, it is important to remember that it matters whether the aphorism is stated in a scholarly context or in an everyday context, and these two contexts should not be confused. What is stated in this paragraph concerns a scholarly context, and the spirit of the aphorism definitely has practical value and utility when it is stated or applied in an everyday context. It is reasonable to just believe in someone who says that they ate a pizza yesterday, whereas it is not reasonable to just believe in someone who says that a pill that they are trying to sell us will make us grow a third arm out of our back. Demanding a scientific degree of evidence for all mundane claims in our everyday life would make living much more of an inconvenient challenge than it needs to be, and not demanding a scientific degree of evidence for extraordinary sounding claims in an everyday context would make us gullible and therefore easily fooled, scammed, or manipulated.

In light of all of these considerations, what about if we do change it up a few notches, and now there is a shining pink elephant that is being reported to exist in the room. Clearly this would cause a lot more a priori skepticism in the rest of us, since while there are a few rare cases of pink elephants found in nature, never do they shine their hue in a blinding manner. How many randomly selected people going in with various devices like metal detectors, DNA analysis kits, large CT scanners, etc., to verify that this shining pink elephant is real would it require? When one thousand randomly selected people all come back saying the same thing, do we start trusting them? Can we then say that we know there is a shining pink elephant in that room? I think some people would still remain skeptical, whether that skepticism was justified or not. The story spreads, and people wish that they get a chance to verify for themselves. And some do, as many of the next nine thousand randomly selected people going in will be skeptical and very eager to see for themselves, feel the elephant, ride it, look for deceptive machines that may be the cause of this elephant and its luminosity, etc. And yet, all of a sudden we are at ten thousand randomly selected people who all firmly, convincingly, sincerely, and justifiably maintain that there really is a shining pink elephant in that room.

Many people testify that they were just as skeptical as you and me before having had this experience of going into the room, and yet their skepticism was quelled by their experience. The number multiplies, and suddenly we are at one hundred thousand randomly selected people, all having the same experience of this room. While surely there are quite a few untrustworthy, gullible, irrational, or delusional people in the population, it is very far from one hundred percent of us, which leads us to the crucial question that we all need to ask ourselves:

What rational reason can we possibly have for thinking that it is not beyond astronomically likely that our own skepticism would encounter the same fate as everyone else's?

This is figuratively and roughly the epistemic situation that we actually are in with regard to profound NDEs. That is, if we for the sake of focusing only on this thought experiment completely disregard the evidence from the empirical investigation of the NDE that helps to verify the survivalist interpretation of the NDE from a scientific point of view, such as evidence of people accurately reporting what was occurring in the operating room while their brains were demonstrably flat-lined during cardiac arrest.[24] Additionally, NDErs also come back with a lot of noticeable and objectively measurable aftereffects from the NDE that people who come out of the room presumably would not have from seeing, observing, and confirming the existence of a shining pink elephant in the room. While it is the combination of that kind of scientific evidence with the philosophical argument presented in this book that provides the strongest grounds for understanding and concluding that it is extremely likely that an afterlife exists in light of all the data we have on NDEs, this book only focuses on presenting and arguing for the latter.

People who are representative of the population as a whole are in large numbers having an experience where it is not just deeply unmissable and self-evident that something seems to exist, but that it is also completely justifiably being realized as really being there (which will be demonstrated in the next chapter). At the same time, that the thing not just seems to exist but is also actually there and justifiably realized as such admittedly does sound hard to believe in for the rest of us who have not had that experience, and the implications thereof are also extremely controversial, taboo, and unmentionable in society in general and especially so in academia.[25] Another similarity worth mentioning is that the randomly selected people entering the room do not know how the shining pink elephant came to be or how it got in there, they just justifiably know that it is undeniably and truly there. Similarly, NDErs generally do not come back knowing why the afterlife exists or how all of creation actually came to be in the first place, they just justifiably know that an afterlife actually and undeniably exists. We have millions of people who are representative of the population as a whole who are either going through the initial stages of the dying process and who are being resuscitated back to life from it, or who come close to death in general and get medical intervention before the onset of cardiac arrest, who are reporting what it is like to have a lucid experience while this is happening, and that there really is an external reality to this one. Furthermore, this has likely been happening for thousands of years as well, as the first recorded NDE, even if fictional, is to be found in the writings of Plato.[26] Ever since, NDEs have been documented to transpire throughout all of history[27] to people who are representative of the population as a whole and therefore also are of all ages[28] from all over the world,[29] which clearly makes the idea of an ancient and global conspiracy to account for all of these testimonies seem extremely unlikely. These people who are representative of the population as a whole are reporting that it not just appears to be an external reality (that they might have been fooled into accepting by their brain going haywire), but are intersubjectively agreeing with each other about the fact that there really is one and that this experience eradicated all conceivable doubt in their minds of this fact. Here are some illustrative quotes from NDErs themselves:

"[I]n addition to having no belief and no faith, I don't have any doubt. I am doubtless and completely unafraid of death because I know where I'm going. ... So I don't have to believe that this glass exists, and that water exists, you know we take it for granted we know it exists, that was the same way, a similar way to which the divine presented itself as self-evidently so."[30]

"I no longer viewed death in the same way as others did, either, so it was very hard for me to mourn anyone. Of course, if someone close to me passed on, I was sad because I missed them. But I no longer mourned for the deceased, because I knew they'd transcended to another realm, and I knew that they were happy! It's not possible to be sad there. ... I now hold a view of life that very few, if any, in my social circle shared or even related to. ... I was also finding it challenging to integrate back into life because this world still didn't seem real to me. The other realm felt more genuine."[31]

"Now, you know, us who've had a near-death, we know our truth. We know, like I know what happens when you die. I know where you go, I know what it feels like, I know what heaven is, if you want to call it that. I have all this awareness that is embodied in my being, that I came back with."[32]

"In a moment I was just somewhere else. ... I certainly understand people's skepticism about this. If it hadn't happened to me, I'd be skeptical about it too. Was I just suffering from ... oxygen starvation of the brain? Was this something that could have brought about this hallucination? ... That was the real world there. You know, that was really home. ... The fear of death is certainly gone, and when it comes my time to go, I'm ready. ... It has changed my entire life, it changed the way I felt about how I wanted to live my life, how I wanted to fit in."[33]

"I was standing in a mist and I knew immediately that I had died. And I was so happy that I had died but I was still alive. And I can't tell you how I felt. It was, 'Oh, God, I'm dead, but I'm here. I'm me.['] And I started pouring out these enormous feelings of gratitude because I still existed and yet I knew perfectly well that I had died."[34]

"I **know** there is life after death. Nobody can shake my belief. I have *no doubt—it's peaceful and nothing to be feared."*[35] (emphasis in original)

"Upon entering that Light... the atmosphere, the energy, it's total pure energy, it's total knowledge, it's total love—everything about it is definitely the afterlife[.]"[36]

"It gave me an answer to what I think everyone must wonder about at one time or another in this life. Yes, there is an afterlife! More beautiful than anything you can begin to imagine. Once you know it, there is nothing that can equal it. You just know!"[37]

"Everybody is [going to] experience what I experienced, at some point. Most of the time people don't come back from that, it's called dying."[38]

"Like a lot of people, for most of my life I was terrified of death. ... I basically learned a fear of death, I was terrified that what it meant was, you know, blackness, the end of consciousness forever, there was nothing, you know, that was [going to] be it, and I was so terrified of that concept that I really couldn't live. I mean it was hobbling me, it was draining me. ... [M]oving into that atheist/agnostic space as a young adult, you know, I just didn't know what came after. ... I have absolutely zero fear of death now, because I know it's not really the end. You know, it's just a transition, and that's it."[39]

The literature on NDEs is filled with testimonies of this kind. These testimonies clearly illustrate how NDErs interpreted their NDE, the certainty they now have from having had one, and how that manifests in other ways in how they relate to life and death accordingly. Of course, NDErs do not just say that they are now convinced that an afterlife exists after their NDE, but also live their lives differently and behave in a way that one might presume would follow from and being consistent with actually being convinced that an afterlife exists.[40] A good illustration of this is how NDErs very frequently lose their fear of death. Here are some illustrative quotes from NDErs themselves:

"If this is what death is like, then I'm not afraid to go ... I have absolutely no fear at all."[41]

"I have no fear of death."[42]

"I'm not afraid of death at all."[43]

"Well, I certainly have no fear of death."[44]

"I had been terrified of death before, it [the NDE] left me with a total lack of fear of death."[45]

"I have no fear of death. I don't to this day."[46]

"I'm not afraid of dying. I'm really not afraid and I used to be scared to death."[47]

"I know a lot of people have a fear of death. I have zero fear of death."[48]

"But there's such a wonderful world on the other side, and it's nothing to fear, and it's actually really... I can't wait, but, you know, it's not my time yet either, I got more work to do here."[49]

"I know that consciousness survives the death of the physical body because I've had that experience personally. ... Having had this NDE, I no longer fear death. ... [W]hen my time comes, I will embrace death. In fact, I know people who are dying right now and I envy them their journey. It's a wonderful, wonderful place

to go. But, I just don't like being left behind. I don't think any of us do."[50]

Quotes like these clearly illustrate how NDErs generally lose their fear of death completely. Indeed, the literature on NDEs is overflowing with quotes like these, just like it is overflowing with quotes about how the NDE changed the NDErs' views on survival and the existence of an afterlife, and this is how one NDE researcher illustrates all of these points concisely:

> *[M]y respondents now believe in life after death, and base that belief on their own experience, which in many cases explicitly contradicts the views held earlier.*
>
> *Over three-quarters of my respondents said that they had a fear of death before the NDE, whereas not one person among my sample has a fear of death now. Many laughed at the question.*[51]

Given that NDEs are an abstract concept that is hard to relate to for most people who have not had them, however, it is much easier to use the analogy of a physical and well-protected room to think about, conceptualize, and relate to the epistemic situation that we are finding ourselves in with respect to NDEs and NDErs. So in the same way that we have no reason to doubt the existence of the shining pink elephant in the room when everyone who has had an opportunity to investigate its existence has come to the same conclusion, so too do we have no reason to doubt the existence of an afterlife when everyone who has had the opportunity to investigate its existence firsthand has come to the conclusion that it is there.

Or do we? And if so, for what relevant, rational, dispassionate, and nonideological reason? The existence of an afterlife does not necessarily contradict anything else we know about the world,[52] so how is the claim of the existence of an afterlife possibly justified as being so extraordinary that millions of people who are representative of the population as a whole and who are all agreeing that it is there, based on their direct experience of it, still insufficient to infer its beyond astronomically likely existence? We already know that if we did not have an incredulous reaction to the claim on a psychological level, or if we were not emotionally reluctant to accept it due to our worldview-preserving defense mechanisms, or if we were not unfamiliar with or bad at imagining what having an NDE is like, or if we were not reluctant to publicly recognize the truth of the claim due to the academic peer pressure to believe in its negation,[53] it would be extremely obvious that the claim was extremely likely to be true. This is plainly obvious with the scenario of the brown table with a white plate on it in the room, even with just a thousand testimonies by randomly selected people, and none of the reasons just listed are empirically or rationally valid justifications for thinking that an otherwise well-supported claim is less likely to be true. But if millions or tens of millions of people who are representative of the population as a whole are supposedly still not enough for some reason, what if it were hundreds of millions of people who were representative of the population as a whole reporting that there is an afterlife due to their profound NDEs? Billions? What if every single person on Earth had a profound NDE except for one person, would that still be insufficient for that person to come to the conclusion that it is beyond astronomically likely that there is an afterlife? Of course some of those with a skepticism of solipsistic proportions will unreflectively laugh at the idea at first, but once again it is worth emphasizing that it is not one hundred percent certainty of the logical proof kind akin to "I doubt, therefore I think, therefore I exist" that is being claimed here, only certainty of a more empirical nature.

While the existence of an afterlife does not necessarily imply that anything else we know about the world through science has to be wrong, as both the laws of physics and the findings of neuroscience are completely compatible with its possible existence,[54] it is still important to ask the following question: Even if the laws of physics as we currently understand them were reported to be violated outright in that room, would we still have any reason to doubt what everyone reported? Among such a huge cohort of millions of randomly selected people, there are at least tens of thousands of realistic and extremely skeptical people, scientists, engineers, and philosophers, etc., who would be more than qualified and eager to disagree with the narrative if they found any reason to do so – and yet they did not. The inevitable conclusion is that since we have no reason to think that our own skepticism would not meet the same fate as theirs were we to go into that room and investigate for ourselves, we have no justifiable reason to sustain our own skepticism in the first place.

If this sounds outrageously unrealistic or even downright insane to some people, to give up on something so extremely well-established as the laws of physics as we currently understand them in light of the reported findings in this room, then we once again just increase the numbers to properly illustrate the force of the argument. While we already know from the prior patterns that this trend will continue forever to any number, let us make it a theoretical reality and go from 10^7 to roughly 7.8×10^9, or everyone but ourselves. If everyone in the whole world except for ourselves went into that room and saw this abnormality for themselves, and changed their views on reality accordingly after concluding that there really was a metaphorical black swan to the laws of physics as we currently understand them in that room, what would be our reasoning for thinking that they are not qualified to make that observation? What understanding do we have that they do not have, or did not take into consideration when doing their investigation? Surely it is not reasonable to insist that we alone understand the necessity of eternally clinging to the belief in the laws of physics as we currently understand them, come what may, better than all other scientists and great thinkers in the world. Can it truthfully be argued that they are not as well acquainted as we are with all the reasons we have (and they had) for doubting what everyone observes in that room? After all, a lot of people understand why the laws of physics as we currently understand them are so well-established in the first place, and why someone not familiar with the findings in that room would be highly a priori skeptical of such a claim. No one who has been inside of that room would deny that the laws of physics appear to be universal outside of that room, but nevertheless they maintain that this one abnormality was definitely real and unexplainable with the hitherto accepted theories. Therefore, they were all forced to change their worldview in light of what they unearthed in that room, even if they can not necessarily explain everything about the abnormality.

The percentage of trustworthy people in the population is probably largely independent of the content that is reported to exist in the room, save for the consideration that it might be easier for many people to convincingly lie about something mundane existing or happening in the room than it might be to convincingly lie about something extraordinary existing or happening in the room. However, the same might not be true for what the percentage of people is who are qualified to investigate and confirm the existence of whatever seems to be in there. For instance, investigating and confirming that a brown table with a white plate on it really is there and really is made of the materials that it appears to be made of might be easier for more people than to confirm that a shining pink elephant really is there, or that the laws of physics might really be violated. But in either scenario, people can bring with them tools to find out everything that they need to check, which for instance can be a computer with an offline version of Wikipedia, or with entire digital libraries of books on it. Even many who do not have the necessary education in science, technology, or engineering, etc., could therefore easily search around to find out what kind of tests they would need to do to be justifiably certain of what they experienced in there. Indeed, once word started to spread about what was reported to justifiably exist in there by the first randomly selected people going in, others on the outside could easily make a checklist and instruction manual for all the tools that should be brought into the room, and for all the tests that should be done by the randomly selected people who are next in line to go in there. This way, they would know what they should expect to find when doing those tests if the thing reported to be in there really is in there, and what they should expect to find if it is actually not, and they would not need to waste any time figuring it out while they are still in the room. So as exponentially more randomly selected people enter the room, we can be exponentially more certain that at least some of them are able and willing to follow basic instructions of what to do, and what counterarguments to take into consideration and test for.

Just like the randomly selected people who observed, thoroughly confirmed, and hence justifiably know that the laws of physics are violated in the room are forced to abandon their former worldview in light of what they learned during their experience of the room, so too is the same thing true for everyone who observes, thoroughly confirms, and justifiably knows that an afterlife exists during their NDE. Many NDErs understand the general idea of the suggestion that brain chemistry might have been responsible for their experience somehow, and a very small and informed minority of NDErs understand all, many, or at least some of the various psychological or psychophysiological arguments of oxygen starvation, endogenous DMT dump, wishful thinking, etc., that have been proposed as alternative explanations for the NDE. And just like many people in the general population, many NDErs are also aware of the exceedingly intimate relationship between mental states and brain states in everyday life. The experience itself, however, was obviously and outright incompatible to the NDEr with the notion that it was generated by the brain. To understand how they can be so certain of this when it appears at first glance to be such a natural and obvious explanation to many who have not had the experience, we must first ask ourselves why we are certain of anything regarding this earthly everyday reality in the first place.

Chapter 4

Realer Than Real

Everyday life is clearly some kind of experience that we are currently having. Likewise, dreams are some kind of experience that people often have, and NDEs are some kind of experience that people who are representative of the population as a whole sometimes have. In all three cases, some kind of consciousness is having some kind of experience. The Chinese philosopher Zhuangzi, however, once noted that he could not tell whether he was a man dreaming he was one night a butterfly, or if he was that butterfly dreaming forever after that he was a man.[55] And it does raise very relevant questions: How do we determine what is real? By what criteria should we trust in certain experiences more than other experiences? More pertinently, why do we consider daily life as human beings more real than the dreams we have at night? The only answer I can imagine is that we are forced to go on what feels and seems more real, what is coming across as more lucid, vivid, intense, powerful, direct, tangible, coherent, rational, reasonable, clear-thinking, structured, detailed, epistemic, consistent, and contextual, etc. In other words, the experience of everyday life comes across and is experienced as vastly more impressive in all phenomenological qualities. To the vast majority of people, what they experience when they are awake comes across as seeming and feeling more real to them in every single way than the dreams they have at night, and this is the implicit reasoning they use for determining that this human reality is more real.

Let us reverse the issue, and imagine that we were to awaken to a higher reality than this one. How would we go about recognizing it as such? What criteria would we be forced to use for determining this, to make sure that we are not just dreaming or hallucinating from the perspective of this reality as human beings?

Unless there are mechanisms beyond my imagination that such a higher reality could employ for convincing newcomers of its metaphysical supremacy, we would be forced to use the same tools we use here for determining that daily life is more real than our dreams. That is, the new reality should seem and feel more real than this one, and it should come across and be experienced as more impressive in all phenomenological qualities. If it should fail to provide us with such phenomenological differences, like in the movies *The Matrix* and *Inception*, and in Nick Bostrom's simulation argument[56] and similar simulation arguments, where the different levels of reality are all perceived and felt as roughly equally real, it would be reasonable to remain skeptical for quite a while.

As an aside and before moving on, however, it is interesting to note that in the movies *The Matrix*, *Inception*, and in Nick Bostrom's simulation argument, and in many simulation discussions that are going on in the philosophical zeitgeist, it is often assumed that the higher reality that we come from operates by largely the same laws of physics as we do, or is similar in many other ways. This is evidenced by the fact that the cause of the simulation from the perspective of the higher reality is often that of them mastering the computational technology necessary to manipulate the seat of consciousness in nearly any way desired. But in fact, just like we might be in a situation like the aforementioned scenarios, we might also be under the influence of a drug in a higher reality, or under a wizard's spell, or we might be a stone, a star, or a vacuum of 3.29 m^3 in a vat – no need even for a brain, or even matter. That is what many of us think generate consciousness in this reality, but there is nothing to suggest it is applicable to any higher reality, since there is no reason to think that their reality is defined in any way by the same or similar parameters as ours. And if down the line we are able to create simulations ourselves, why replicate the parameters of this existence if we could create anything, including endless paradises, or fantasy or science fiction worlds? Put another way, why should all the turtles share the same or similar parameters, either up or down? This extreme lack of imagination seems to me to be one of the main reasons why simulation arguments that entertain higher realities similar to this one are taken a lot more seriously than the afterlife argument, even though that too is a simulation argument. Why is it that the one simulation argument we actually have evidence of, via millions of justified testimonies by people who are representative of the population as a whole to its effect, is the one that contemporary philosophers take the least serious?

These peculiarities of contemporary philosophers aside, however, let us move on. If the experience of the new reality should not fail to provide us with the aforementioned phenomenological differences, and if it instead should succeed in providing us with a reality that seems and feels more real in every way than the one we came from, and if it would do all of this in a convincing manner, would we have any reason not to trust it? Would it always be more reasonable to sit and shake in a corner, repeating to ourselves that it just has to be the delusions of a mind trapped in a seemingly lower reality for trillions of years? At some point, it has to be conceded that if a reality feels, seems, and appears more real in every conceivable way than the one we came from, and it can be explained and shown to us in every way why we thought the lower reality was the primary reality while we were there, then the only rational conclusion is that the new reality we are encountering is the more real reality.

This is precisely the situation that NDErs are finding themselves in, and they are sure for these precise reasons that they have indeed seen the real world or a higher reality during their NDE and not just hallucinated it all. I will provide a few quotes to illustrate what NDErs generally have to say on this issue, both from NDErs and from NDE researchers:

"*Interviewer: 'Silly question, but I'm sure there were professionals out there in the mental health field and physical health field who questioned whether or not this was a figment of your imagination, a dream, a hallucination, or something even more profound than that?'*

NDEr: 'Yeah, my doctors did it.'

Interviewer: 'And how have you reconciled those questions?'

NDEr: 'I don't care what they think. One of the commonalities among the near-death experience accounts that I have read, of those who have gotten far enough into the experience, is that the sense of reality there far, far outweighs the sense of reality we have here. I mean, looking back at human life from that vantage point I could not believe that I had ever thought this was real. And so the same sense of unreality that we get about dreams while we're here in human form, I had while I was there about human life. So there is no doubt in my mind that it was real, and that's true reality. This is a virtual reality game, a role, a play, a dream, an illusion, a character that I'm playing.'"[57]

"*How real was it? It was so real that nothing in this life… It's as if that was in a magnificent color movie and everything I'm looking at is in black and white now. It's that vivid. Recently I had a conversation with a friend and he said, and we were talking about this, and he said to me, 'Well, you just think it happened.' I said, 'No, I know it happened.' And he said, 'Well, you think it happened.' I said, 'Okay, I'll agree with you, as long as you understand that I think we're having this conversation, and I think that happened much more clearly than I think we're having this conversation.'*"[58]

"I'm still trying to fit it in with this dream that I'm walking around in, in this world. The reality of the experience is undeniable. This world that we live in, this game that we play called life is almost a phantom in comparison to the reality of that."[59]

"[T]he physical [world] resembled a black and white movie in comparison with the world in front of me[.] ... That's what it felt like, waking up from a dream, waking up to who I truly am and this life was nothing but a dream[.]"[60]

"So I was being drawn towards this light, and I was being pulled and pulled and pulled. And I was almost to the light, and basically what it felt like was waking up. Like, this existence here on this Earth was just a dream that I had had, and I was waking up, and I was more alive and alert than I have ever been in my life."[61]

This is how one NDE researcher characterized the stereotypical response from NDErs to the suggestion that their experience was like a dream:

"Dream? I am more sure that I was there, than when I went to the supermarket today to get a Coke. I am more sure I was there. [It was] the most real experience [I have] ever had."[62]

Another NDE researcher describes thusly what one NDEr told her about how the NDE was realer than real, and also notes how NDErs often describe their NDEs:

"[H]e answered the question of the reality of the experience, and he said, and this is a quote, it's obviously stuck with me for like forty years. He said: 'That experience was realer than sitting here writing this response to you.' So the experience was realer than real. That's actually a phrase that NDErs often use, that the experience is hyperreal, it's hyperlucid, and involves both normal

and supernormal perception."[63]

This is the selection of a few illustrating quotes from two other NDE researchers:

"[M]any people claim that their near-death experiences were 'more real' to them than their usual waking experiences. Among participants in this study, for example, a woman who gave birth under trichloroethylene anesthesia at age 23 said, 'Never, ever, did I think it might have been a dream. I knew that it was true and real, more real than any other thing I've ever known.' A woman who had a pulmonary embolism after a Caesarean delivery at age 31 said, 'My death experience is more real to me than life.' A woman who gave birth prematurely under nitrous oxide anesthesia at age 27 said, 'It was more real than real: absolute reality.' A 29-year-old woman said, 'There was no sense of doubt whatsoever. Everything had a sense of being "more real" than anything that would normally be experienced in the physical world as we know it.' A man who rolled his car over at the age of 21 said, 'I have no doubt that this experience was real. It was vastly more real than anything we experience here.' A woman who attempted suicide at the age of 31 said, 'This was more real than anything on Earth. By comparison, my life in my body had been a dream.' And a woman who, at the age of 25, bled out during a surgical procedure when the surgeon accidentally cut an artery, noted: 'What happens during an NDE happens in the realm of truth, in the true reality, and what happens here on Earth is just a dream.'"[64]

In other words, the NDE world comes across as more real and coherent in every way imaginable to the NDEr, and having an NDE has been described as waking up from a deep, deep dream (or nightmare). So contrary to the belief shared by many that death is kind of like an eternal slumber, or that dying is kind of like falling asleep, it seems instead to be the exact opposite.

That is, it seems to be the case according to NDErs that dying is actually like waking up and realizing that life was actually the dream all along in comparison with the self-evident ultrareality that is experienced in the afterlife that NDErs encounter. For all of these reasons and considerations it is therefore extremely important to recognize, understand, and always keep in mind that NDEs are, contrary to popular assumption, the very opposite of dreams. Every reason we have for concluding that this reality is more real than our dreams at night, NDErs have for asserting that the afterlife is more real than this world. That is, these experiences are vastly more impressive in all phenomenological qualities than this experience we are having right now of daily life as human beings. Not surprisingly, then, these experiences are often described with words such as ultrareal and hyperreal, or phrases such as realer than real, and they are very figurative instances of the allegory of the cave, a thought experiment known to all philosophers.

The allegory of the cave can be simplified and summarized like this: Some people are trapped living in a cave, watching shadows of things and believing that those shadows are the real world. One day someone in this cave escapes it, walks out into the light of the sun and sees what is unmistakably the real world in comparison to the world of the shadows in the cave. But upon returning to the cave, eager to tell the good and fascinating news to all their friends, they are to their surprise met with disbelief, ridicule, and even hostility.

Is it not ironic that so many philosophers of our time have completely failed to realize that this is the near-perfect analogy for what is happening with NDErs, and that their own reaction to the idea that the NDE could be seriously regarded as indicative of the existence of an afterlife[65] is that of such a troglodyte? These people who are representative of the population as a whole are reporting in the millions that they have escaped the metaphorical cave of the human experience and experienced an unmistakably higher reality in the light. Furthermore, it is a documented fact that many are treated so harshly upon returning to this world and sharing their experience and the insights that came with it that they sometimes decide that it is pointless or not worth the effort to even try.[66]

All of this is brought up because it is important to realize why NDErs themselves are so sure of their claimed experience of the afterlife, because if they did not have epistemic justification for their newfound convictions it would mean a lot less that they were convinced. The fact that they are coming back saying that due to these reasons they are more sure that they experienced the afterlife than they have ever been sure about anything in this world, however, is as good an epistemic justification as anything (outside of theoretical philosophy) can ever hope to be. To the extent that we are justifiably sure about the existence of this world, NDErs are even more justifiably sure about the existence of the afterlife, since all the reasons we have for being certain of the existence of this world are vastly amplified for the NDEr regarding their reasons for being certain of the existence of an afterlife. What better reason could they possibly have for asserting that their NDE was real and not a brain-generated hallucination, other than the fact that their NDE was vastly more real in every relevant way than the experience of this reality?

The scientific study of NDEs is naturally focusing on verifying things objectively, and that includes trying to verify claims of out-of-body experiences (OBEs) during NDEs. While NDErs' claims of having left their bodies, such as seeing or hearing things that existed or events that transpired in the operating room or in their general proximity, have been documented to transpire as reported quite a few times,[67] we could grant even more impressive scenarios than this. For instance, we could imagine scenarios where NDErs would see or hear everything that existed and was transpiring in the entire hospital they were in, or the entire city they found themselves in, or the entire country they found themselves in, or even the entire world during a time at which they were demonstrably flat-lined during cardiac arrest. If scenarios like these were documented to transpire, it would surely help the rest of us in concluding that NDErs' claims were true a lot more. But it is important to understand that it would not convince the NDErs themselves significantly more.[68] To illustrate why this is the case, let us use the dream analogy again.

Say that we fall asleep, dream some random nonsense, and wake up for a short amount of time. Upon waking up, we remember what we last were dreaming, and when we fall back asleep again, we take with us some observations that we made about that dream in the waking state and continue with the same dream. Say that we had found ourselves in a meadow with some friends in the dream, but could not quite place where it was occurring while in the dream. When we wake up, we realize the physical location of the meadow and what was surrounding it geographically. When we fall back asleep again and continue the same dream, we remember that we woke up and realized these things, and are able to tell our dream character friends all about what was beyond their line of sight, that the meadow was close to a lake in one direction and close to a soccer field in the other direction. When we go on exploring with our friends in the dream, they are all astounded that we could know all of this upon realizing that we were right, and so are we to some extent. But in this state of lucid dreaming, what would convince us more of the fact that we were having a lucid dream: That we were right about the physical location of the meadow in the context of the dream, or that we had perpetual access to the perfect memory of what it was phenomenologically like to wake up? Similarly, when we wake up from a dream about being on a meadow, is the realization of the geographical location of the meadow what convinces us that what we just experienced was just a dream and that what we now experience is a more real reality? It is a part of it, of course, but it is only a tiny part of it. What really convinces us the most by far that what we just experienced was just a dream is the tremendous difference in all of the phenomenological qualities of the experience of being awake as human beings contrasted to the vastly lessened phenomenological qualities of the experience of dreaming.

When we wake up from a dream, it is the enormous difference in the perception and feeling of realness that immediately and justifiably removes all rational doubt that this world is more real than our dreams. When this happens again during an experience of a higher reality than this life, how could it all of a sudden be irrational to have the same reaction with the same epistemic justification? While some would argue that it could be our brains generating an illusory experience of a higher reality,[69] it is important to understand and truly appreciate that this is as unlikely from the perspective of an NDEr as the idea that it is the brains of our dream characters that are currently generating this experience of daily life is unlikely to us, for precisely the same reasons. Our dreams, no matter how phenomenologically impressive or persuasive they may be while we are still in them, are still realized as vastly less phenomenologically impressive than daily life when we wake up from them. Therefore, they are all realized as self-evidently not real when we wake up back to daily life. And the same is true when we wake up from this life during an NDE. No matter how phenomenologically impressive or persuasive all the phenomenological qualities that the experience of this world admittedly is, it is still hardly even comparable to the vastly more impressive degree of all phenomenological qualities of the experience of the NDE world. So to ask NDErs to take seriously the possibility that it might have been their brains fooling them is about as reasonable as asking ourselves to take seriously the notion that it is the brains of our dream characters that are currently fooling us and generating this entire experience of everyday life.

Of course, a statement like that may at first sound completely unrealistic, greatly exaggerated, or even downright insane to many who have not carefully and charitably listened to what NDErs are actually reporting about the differences in realness between the experiences in greater detail. Furthermore, it is not easily denied that the most persuasive arguments against the possible existence of an afterlife are those that deny that consciousness can exist without a functioning biological brain, and the scholars who argue against a survivalist interpretation of NDEs often go out of their way to overemphasize just how impressively and demonstrably interwoven mental events and brain events are in everyday life. For these reasons, it may therefore be useful to elaborate further on what it means that an experience is vastly more lucid, vivid, intense, powerful, direct, tangible, coherent, rational, reasonable, clear-thinking, structured, detailed, epistemic, consistent, and contextual, etc., than another experience.

For instance, some have made the point that the lucidity and vividness of an experience is in itself not a sufficiently good reason to draw any conclusions about the objective reality of an experience, since people can have lucid or unusually vivid dreams.[70] However, this line of reasoning does not take into account the fact that people who have lucid or unusually vivid dreams seldom come back saying that they are afterward convinced that their dreams were more real, lucid, or vivid than the experience of waking life, or even that their dreams were equally as real, lucid, or vivid as the experience of waking life. While dreams may differ in their degree of lucidity, vividness, intensity, or powerfulness, and some dreams are therefore much more lucid, vivid, intense, or powerful than other dreams, all of them still have an overall dreamlike quality to them in all of these phenomenological aspects that can not be compared to the much higher degree of lucidity, vividness, intensity, and powerfulness of the experience of everyday life. Furthermore, our dreams are very intangible and indirect experiences, where our surroundings seem to be more of an abstract idea rather than something that we can concretely touch, feel, and be in direct contact with. This is clearly contrasted with the direct and tangible nature of the experience of everyday life, where we can touch and feel our surroundings much more directly and much more tangibly.

Similarly, dreams are often an incoherent mess of largely random, unspecified, and unintelligible nonsense, where things often do not make much sense even as we are experiencing them, and we often do not have a clear grasp on what is happening or why, and the experience does not come across as a unified whole in a comprehensible way. There is also not much detail, structure, or richness to our experience of the dream scenarios. All of these considerations are unlike the experience of everyday life, which is clearly an experience that is a lot more detailed, structured, coherent, rational, and clear-thinking, where we have a lot more detail, structure, and richness to our experience, and the experience comes across as a lot more coherent and unified, and people usually have some kind of idea of what is going on and can reflect upon their experience a lot more in a clearer way.

Furthermore, dreams are usually very inconsistent, where we are jumping in and out of different scenarios and environments which seem to come into existence on the spot, only to disappear just as fast again. The differences in the consistency and structure of the experience of dreaming and the experience of everyday life is therefore quite self-evident, as the latter is always of the same type. That is, we always wake up as the same character with the same environment that behaves and is structured in the same way all the time, in the same general scenario of being the same creature in the same society on the same planet. Furthermore, all of this is being remembered each and every time we wake up, rather than being realized and learned about from scratch.

Lastly, when we wake up we also realize and understand in what context our previous experiences, our dreams, were happening, that they were created by our physical brains during sleep. Therefore, we can tell that our previous experience of dreaming was occurring in a larger context as a result of something happening in a higher reality, even though it did not seem like it when we were still dreaming. Furthermore, during dreams we are often unable to reflect much upon these dreams or have access to much of our memory.[71] And when we wake up, we are able to remember or realize epistemic details in our waking state that were unavailable to us in our dreams. As the previous example of the meadow and its location illustrated, we can know more about our dream experiences when we enter our everyday life level of reality. These considerations are what is referenced when we say that an experience is more contextual and epistemic than another experience. That is, that the context in which the former experience was ultimately happening in becomes more evident, and we also have access to more knowledge about the experience that we did not have while we were still in the experience, and we also have access to a lot more knowledge in general.

These contrasting and explainable differences between the experience of dreaming and the experience of everyday life are understandable to us, since if for no other reason we have experienced these phenomenological differences firsthand. For NDErs, the discernment that the NDE state of consciousness is more real than our waking state is similarly not arrived at first and foremost through rational reasoning, but is rather an item of direct experience. Intrinsic to waking up in the morning is the experientially self-evident knowledge that the prior state of consciousness, dreaming, is illusory. Similarly, intrinsic to waking up into the NDE state of consciousness is the experientially self-evident knowledge that it is superior to what went before, that is, the experience of everyday life. We do not really reason rationally with ourselves in the morning to find out whether we have awoken to a higher reality than our dreams, and in the same way NDErs do not really reason rationally with themselves to find out whether they have awoken to a higher reality than everyday life in their NDE. Instead, it is just immediately self-evident to NDErs as a matter of direct experience. As a woman who was an atheist prior to her NDE noted:

> *"The minute that I kind of woke up on that hillside in heaven I knew that that was more real than any time I've ever spent here on Earth. ... And I knew instantly that my time here was really but a dream. ... It's real to us when we're in it, but once I was there ... in heaven I realized that's more real, that felt more real, and it made much more sense to me than anything here. This is kind of nonsensical at times. ... In heaven, it's so clear, so real, so rational, so logical, but yet emotional and loving at the same time. Immediately I knew that was real and this was not. Immediately."*[72]

Regardless of whether we consider it a good, a neutral, or a bad thing, however, most of us have not experienced anything like an NDE ourselves, and we will also most likely never do so before our biological lives are permanently over. Furthermore, our imagination is very limited when it comes to trying to imagine what having an NDE is phenomenologically like, and especially when it comes to trying to imagine how it is realer than real. After all, our imagination is generally much less vivid, tangible, real, etc., than the totality of our everyday life experience. So when we try to imagine what having an NDE is phenomenologically like, and especially how it may be realer than real, it can produce a vague inner mental picture that, like all other things we imagine, is much less overall real than our experience of the totality of everyday life. In other words, trying to imagine what having an NDE is phenomenologically like, and especially how NDEs are realer than real, may even end up being counterproductive in terms of helping us appreciate this attribute of the experience. Therefore, to understand the details of the phenomenological differences between the experience of everyday life and the experience of what having an NDE is like as well as NDErs that actually lived those insights, our only option is to try our best to do so on a conceptual level. But as we go about trying to do so, we must keep in mind at all times the difference between trying to imagine what having an NDE is phenomenologically like and understanding what having an NDE is phenomenologically like on a conceptual level.

Perhaps the most conceptually relatable illustration of the difference in vividness between waking life and NDEs is how people have been known to describe more colors, sounds, smells, tastes, sensations, and sometimes even more senses (such as perfect telepathic communication) than are available in everyday life, and also report that the intensity and vividness of all of these sensory inputs are sometimes greatly enhanced. For instance, the deepest of NDErs sometimes make these kinds of comments about these differences:

"He was a concentrated field of energy, radiant in splendor indescribable, except to say goodness and love. This was more loving than one can imagine. I knew that this radiant being was powerful. It was making me feel so good all over. I could feel its light on me – like very gentle hands around me. And I could feel it holding me. But it was loving me with overwhelming power. ... Then he called out in a musical tone to the luminous entities who surrounded the great center. Several came and circled around us. During what follows some came and went but normally there were five or six and sometimes as many as eight with us. ... They said that they could turn their brilliance down and appear as people, and I told them to stay as they were. They were ... beautiful[.] ... As

an aside, I'm an artist. There are three primary, three secondary, and six tertiary colors in the visible light spectrum. Here, I was seeing a visible light spectrum with at least 80 new primary colors. I was also seeing this brilliance. It's disappointing for me to try and describe, because I can't – I was seeing colors that I had never seen before. What these beings were showing me was their glory. ... Everywhere around us were countless radiant beings, like stars in the sky, coming and going. It was like a super magnified view of a galaxy super packed with stars. And in the giant radiance of the center they were packed so densely together that individuals could not be identified."[73]

"There are great cities very similar to the ones we live in now, only these places have great harmony and balance to them. I saw one city that was made entirely of gold and precious stones. It actually glowed! ... The higher up you go in Heaven, the more it becomes impossible to give a human description. I try to explain it by saying there are flashes of [l]ight and brilliant colors of every spectrum everywhere. ... The [r]ealm is a real happening place I can tell you that! I always laugh when I think of society's image of Heaven as little cherubs sitting around playing harps on clouds. ... [I]t's a whole lot more intense than that! ... Surprisingly, texture is apparently something that can be felt in Heaven. In fact, all of our five senses are very much the same as on Earth, only in Heaven, they are far more developed to an unimaginable degree. We have the ability to smell, see, hear, touch (and get ready for this) [- even taste]!"[74]

"The light was so bright that it was brighter than ten thousand suns, and I immediately said, 'This should be burning my retinas.' But it wasn't. It was a gentle but powerful light."[75]

"I did become aware of a point of white light. Intense, intense, brilliant, gajillion times brighter than the Sun, little point of white

light. And ... it was ... absolutely beautiful. It was alive, it was like breathing. ... [W]e were singing, and I'll never forget this, it was so beautiful ... and it makes music as we understand it seem like a cheap imitation. ... [I]t ... took on whole other dimensions[.]"[76]

"The brightest thing that you can imagine is a dark hole compared to the bright light that I saw."[77]

"[T]he first thing that happened when I transitioned into the light was I felt like this bliss, like a sense of peace, ... this divine love was just wrapped around me. ... I knew I was what people say, [that] they're home, yes, that's exactly how you feel, you feel so very safe. And so, as I was in this bliss, and it was like ... I was ... plugged into the motherboard, and you know, I had this expansive experience of, like, everything just ... All your senses are like super sized, ... it was like this infinite divine consciousness. ... [Y]ou really don't have any questions, like you have this knowing. ... [T]he light parted at one point, and I stepped out into like this meadow, and there were trees, and grass, and these, like a field of daisies, and there were beings ... that were in the meadow. ... [A]t that point it was so overwhelming to see it, and to see that perfection[.] ... [B]ut I had this memory of, it was almost like I've been here before. ... [B]ut it was just taking in the beauty of pure perfection."[78]

"It's like living in a two-dimensional black and white world here, ... compared to multicolor, multi-sensory VR immersion there. ... And so once you've been in that place, coming here, as beautiful as it is, and I live in an extraordinarily beautiful place on purpose, so that I can get as close to beauty as I possibly can, but even that it's just, like, 'Oh well, you know, that's really pretty.' But not the same as ultimate divine beauty. ... [Even sunrises] were ugly for a while, ... the first year was very difficult."[79]

"The sound of that music I cannot possibly describe with words because it simply cannot be heard with that clarity in this world[.] ... The colors were out of this world; so deep, so luminous, so beautiful[.] ... My hearing was so acute; I could sense every little detail. ... I was aware of everything around me with so much clarity, every detail, I could see the perfection in every sound[.] ... Totally different perception than the one while in this life. So clear and so secure, alert and conscious of every detail around me[.] ... The colors [were] so vivid, so luminous, so clear, with so much detail[.] ... I could distinguish every detail in that piece of music and with incredible depth[.]"[80]

"I saw the most amazing forest and flowers on the other side. The flowers were all over the place with no resemblance to flowers on [E]arth. Although I can't describe the smell, it was gorgeous! The flowers glowed in different, indescribable colors."[81]

"... I was taken by the hand and led into another realm. It resembled [E]arth because there were trees, sparkling sand, and aquamarine water. There were fruit-laden trees, lush foliage, and vibrantly colored birds. Everything was alive – each flower and every glistening grain of sand. Floral fragrances filled the air."[82]

"[T]he sparkling colors ... were found within and around the strong and pure crystal light that the sky/heavens consisted of. ... We stood there on a high plateau in heavenly beautiful nature. Below to the left was a valley where a river flowed. Further away in the valley, I saw a powerful and clear light that one cannot describe with words. ... The environment was so beautiful that it exceeded human understanding."[83]

"And I realized that he'd been standing in front of a doorway which was transparent, and as I looked through that transparent opening and doorway [there] was an entire new galaxy. A whole new Earth

with a whole new heaven. It was like a parallel universe. As I'm standing there I can see fields and pastures, I can see flowers, I can see grass with light coming off [it]. And so I'm standing there looking at this, 'Incredible, look at this paradise!' ... I can see a crystal clear river, trees along its banks, valleys, mounds in the distance. As I'm standing there I'm thinking, 'I belong here.'"[84]

"In the room were three beings, made of shimmering crystal. Light shone through them like a glass prism, forming a rainbow. ... [P]ure light shone through the fibers, forming colors in all shades. When they spoke, their messages were sent telepathically. They could read my thoughts. ... Looking into their eyes, they were shades of intense colors that changed and shifted with electric sparks. ... And the love radiated from their eyes, as if I were the most precious creation God had ever placed into existence. It was as if they knew me intimately, yet I didn't feel uncomfortable feeling that they did."[85]

"Now, what heaven looks like? 'O m g' doesn't even describe how beautiful this place is. Heaven is, there are no words. I mean, I could sit here ... and just not say anything and just cry, and that would be what heaven looks like. ... There are mountains of beauty, there are things in this realm, you can't even describe how beautiful this place is. There are colors you can't even imagine, there are sounds you can't even create. There are beauties upon this world that you think are beautiful here. Amplify it over there times a billion. There are, it's incredibly beautiful, there's no words to describe how beautiful this place is, it's incredibly gorgeous."[86]

As can be seen by testimonies like these, the extreme beauty and vividness that is experienced in an NDE far surpasses anything that we can even begin to imagine here. And it is worth pointing out and emphasizing that it is not just the NDE as a whole that is more vivid, but also the environment and the beings we encounter and interact with there. That is, the environment and the beings encountered in the NDE world are experienced as far more beautiful and vividly real than our environment and our fellow human beings (and animals) are experienced as beautiful and vividly real in our current everyday life experience.

When it comes to the intensity and powerfulness of the experience, some have made the point that the difference in powerfulness can be illustrated by how being in the light in an NDE is like being in or near a waterfall,[87] which is generally a more powerful experience than, for instance, being in a quiet room. But perhaps the most conceptually relatable illustration of this phenomenological difference is the range and intensity of our emotions. This is how NDErs typically describe these differences:

"... I saw the white light, which was, you know, the best experience I've ever had. Like, basically, all the love that ever was, and all the love that ever will be, forever, for all of eternity, literally being poured onto me like a waterfall. ... I'm literally saying that's what it was. Like a lot of people who have had similar experiences have had difficulty describing this feeling that they received, but that's actually, that's as accurate of a description that I can actually give. ... It was as if I was the last ... living baby in the entire universe left alive, that's how much love there was. It was indescribable."[88]

"Anybody who's ever gone into the light comes back to talk about this ... unconditional love and bliss that they experienced in the light. ... Most people when they describe it, they say it's the most incredible ... loving experience, they feel full of love and what I experienced, it was kind of like, it was almost as if I had turned into champagne, and I was bubbling. You know like my molecules were bubbling and love was going through my molecules and then coming back out from them. And when people describe that, they say it's the most incredible thing in the world. Well it is, but,

it gets better. ... Merging into the source was the most intense experience I had ever had. And that is one of the attributes of unconditional love, its intensity. The emotions that we have when we're out of these bodies are far more intense than everything we ever experience in the body. The bodies really filter out a lot of emotions that we're capable of. ... Have you ever been moved to tears by something? Like maybe by love, or beauty, or gratitude? Or just had that feeling where you were just so moved that you literally cried? You know how strong and vibrant that is, and how cleansing and all-consuming it can be? The unconditional love that we feel in the afterlife is like a hundred or a thousand times more intense than that. Take that feeling and take away the tears and substitute joy, and so make it a joyous love ... that you're feeling[.] ... And that will give you a tiny little taste of what unconditional love feels like."[89]

"There are no words to explain some of the things I saw, felt, experienced. ... There are no words for the feelings I felt. They are too extreme in comparison, to merely be a comparison[.] ... I was not happy, I was a feeling a trillion times more than happy, indescribable to be honest."[90]

"And a lot of experiencers talk about love, about this being a place of love, and I've tried to think of adjectives to describe this, the intensity of this love, you know. Unconditional, pure, powerful. The only one that I can think of that works is infinite. It was infinite. ... It was infinite love. If you can imagine your baby that you love, imagine like the most intense feeling of love you've ever had, your mother, or your dog, whatever, whatever it is, imagine that ... infinite! No end. So powerful and so absorbing. Wave after wave after wave of cleansing white love washing over me, and I became, I was the light. It was so beautiful, it was so beautiful."[91]

"... I saw that I was comprised of billions and billions of colorful

light filled atomic cells. As the [l]ight around me came forward the atom cells in me started to dance and vibrate as if they were being made to magnetically respond to the ever glowing illumination that was increasing and filling the room by the second. Needless to say, the happiness I felt as this happened was indescribable! ... As far as how it feels to be in the presence ... simply consider the most pure state of bliss you can possibly think of and multiply that times any number you could come up with[.]"[92]

"So I went into the light, and as I was moving up into the light, I just started to feel so good. You know like I can't, words can't explain it. Like the higher that I went into the light, and the more that I moved up and further away from Earth, the better I felt. And the feeling of pleasure does not really apply to this Earth, like nothing can compare. Like if you took everything that you were in favor of, like maybe getting a massage, in a hot tub, your favorite music, your favorite food, your favorite drink, everything that you love, happening to you all at once, no matter what it is, all at once, it would not even closely compare to the pleasure that was just within that light. And as you moved further into, like further away from this Earth, the pleasure felt even better. So you just moved up it felt better and better, it was insane."[93]

"If I lived a billion years more, in my body or yours, there's not a single experience on Earth that could ever be as good as being dead. Nothing."[94]

As NDE researcher Kenneth Ring related what one NDEr told him about this issue:

"One person said that if you took the thousand best things that ever happened to you and multiply them by a million, then maybe you'd have some idea of what this experience feels like. It's just totally, totally off the continuum of ordinary human experience according

to these accounts, which are generally stated in very superlative and possibly to our ordinary understanding exaggerated terms. But it seems very faithful to the experience as far as these people are concerned. "[95]

One NDE researcher made a presentation in 2010 where he had found that 56% of all NDErs said that the sensation of the experience contrasted to everyday life was "a thousand times stronger or beyond,"[96] and I have anecdotal familiarity with these kinds of descriptions as well. For instance, one NDEr who had also tried the psychoactive drug MDMA (usually referred to as ecstasy) described to me their NDE as if a million times what the ordinary dosage of this drug provides would not even begin to scratch the surface of explaining the intensity and powerfulness of the love, peace, and bliss that was within the NDE light. While quantifying and comparing the intensity and powerfulness of our emotions may be a difficult thing to do objectively or relatably, there seems to be a nearly indescribable degree of difference between the relatively limited bliss and love we are capable of experiencing in everyday life, contrasted to the intensity and powerfulness of our emotions in an NDE.

Our experience of everyday life is mediated by our sensory organs and our brains interpreting the inputs from those organs, so even though the experience of everyday life does feel very direct and tangible to us, it goes through at least two mediating processes before we experience it. Contrast this with an NDE, where things are experienced directly, without any filters. Robert Perry illustrates this point very well:

... I suspect that a significant part of the conviction is a sense of being in more direct than normal contact with the supposed afterlife environment. In normal life, directness of contact is a major factor in how much people trust their perceptions. To read a story is less convincing than to watch a film, which in turn is

less convincing than to see with one's own eyes. As the directness of contact increases, so does trust in what one perceives. In this world, however, that directness is always limited. People experience the environment through a double filter — the filter of the senses compounded by the filter of interpretations. In many NDEs, however, one gets the sense that this filtering is at least reduced, so that contact is genuinely more direct. One thinks, for instance, of the common claim that communication on the "other side" is done telepathically rather than by speech, so that misunderstandings are largely or completely eliminated. Here, then, is a claim of greater directness that appears to result in greater reality contact. Then there are those cases in which an NDEr claims to have experienced unmediated union with the divine, which, if true, would mean that the normal filtering is not just reduced but is gone. Perhaps this notion of more direct contact helps explain the ... NDE environment being much more self-evident than this world.[97]

Here are some NDErs who more concretely talk about how the NDE is more direct and tangible than everyday life:

*"The sound was palpable and almost material, like a rain that you can feel on your skin but that doesn't get you wet. Seeing and hearing were not separate in this place where I now was. I could **hear** the visual beauty of the silvery bodies of those scintillating beings above, and I could see the surging, joyful perfection of what they sang. It seemed that you could not look at or listen to anything in this world without becoming a part of it — without joining with it in some mysterious way. Again, from my present perspective, I would suggest that you couldn't look **at** anything in that world at all, for the word **at** itself implies a separation that did not exist there. Everything was distinct, yet everything was also a part of everything else, like the rich and intermingled designs on Persian carpet ... or a butterfly's wing. ... Thoughts entered me directly. But it wasn't thought like we experience on earth. It*

wasn't vague, immaterial, or abstract. These thoughts were solid and immediate—hotter than fire and wetter than water—and as I received them I was able to instantly and effortlessly understand concepts that would have taken me years to fully grasp in my earthly life."[98] (emphasis in original)

"It was a total immersion in light, brightness, warmth, peace, security. ... I just immediately went into this beautiful, bright light. It's difficult to describe. In matter of fact, it's impossible to describe. Verbally it can not be expressed. It's something which becomes you, and you become it. I could say that I was peace, I was love, I was the brightness. It was part of me."[99]

"And as I approached the light it got bigger, and more intense, and more beautiful, and more loving, and it sucked me in and absorbed me, and I became the light, and the light became me. I was the white light."[100]

"... I look down and I see myself standing in a very gentle river, and all around me is a very beautiful, very peaceful forest. And this is where it gets hard to describe because it was a rush of all, it was everything wrapped into one. ... And feeling immense awe and bliss and love and relief. ... And there was no other being in my NDE, it was just me, but I didn't feel at all alone. It was the least alone I've ever been in my life. It was like the place itself was alive, and it was telling me things and it was loving me."[101]

"I mean I was free. I was absolutely free and I was immediately greeted by a group of, I don't know what ... people, spirits, beings. For me they had physical form, somewhat three-dimensional, head, arms, legs, wearing these incredible robes and really just, obviously radiant from within, not like there was a sun or bright light shining, but from within and ... it was as though these robes were, I don't know, woven together with fibers of love. I mean, it

was ... a love that is not something we experience here. And it's a love that is pure and complete and **tangible***. You can feel it, you can see it, you can touch it.*"[102] (emphasis in original)

"To my surprise, and also distress, they seemed to be capable of knowing everything I was thinking. I didn't know whether I would be capable of controlling my thoughts and keeping anything secret. We began to engage in thought exchange, conversation that was very natural, very easy and casual. I heard their voices clearly and individually. They each had a distinct personality with a voice, but they spoke directly to my mind, not my ears. ... Everything I thought, they knew. They all seemed to know and understand me very well and to be completely familiar with my thoughts and my past. I didn't feel any desire to ask for someone I had known because they all knew me. Nobody could know me any better. ... Their love was tangible. You could feel it on your body, you could feel it inside you; their love went right through you. I wish I could explain it to you, but I can't."[103]

"[This being] knows my thought before I even speak, it's as though he can read everything within me, nothing is hidden from him. ... As I saw a man's bare feet, dazzling white garments reaching down towards his ankles, as I quickly lifted my face up I could see the chest of a man with his arms outstretched towards me, and out of his face ... pure light. I stood in incredible amazement of the beauty of [this being]. His face was so bright that as you looked into it, it was like you were looking into eternity. It was the form of a man but the face of god. So he puts his presence around me, his arms, so I feel the embrace ... You are ruined for life. For the good, ... the love of [this being] then encompasses who you are."[104]

"I merged with the light, and became it. It was me, and I was it, without differentiation. ... Before me appeared a magnificent being radiating forth pure [d]ivine [l]ove. This being was formless

and was softly and ethereally pulsating, yet somehow it seemed to have a hint of form, [like] a blended, ever-so-faint outline that was even more radiantly brilliant (though, paradoxically, of the same brilliance as all else around it). ... We all shared this intense feeling of [love]. Our communication was silent, absent of words, telepathic. This form of communication was all-knowing, like windows into the heart of the soul, through which the communication expanded both outward and inward. We read one another's thoughts instantaneously. There was no room for even a smidgen of miscommunication. The whole picture of each expression was perfect. The three beings and I expressed everything so clearly, succinctly, and eloquently. The thought-forms flowed back and forth simultaneously, all at once. We all heard one another."[105]

As evidenced by testimonies like these, it seems that we can be even more immersed in the NDE world than we can be even here in our daily waking life, and in the NDE world even our feelings and thoughts can be tangible in a way that they are not in everyday life. In other words, in an NDE we can not just be vastly more immersed with the environment of the NDE world, but also with the beings we encounter there in ways that we can not even imagine what it is like here. That is, the environment and the beings in the NDE world can be far more tangible than the environment and our fellow human beings (and animals) are here, and we can be far more in direct contact with them than we are here. In other words, we are immersed with the environment and the beings there in such a way that we can have instant and flawless telepathic communication with the environment and the beings, but we can also be one with, and completely in direct contact with, the environment and the beings. Additionally, the environment and the beings in the NDE world, including the emotions we have for each other and even our thoughts, are all far more tangible there than they are here.

As can be seen with the phenomenological differences elaborated upon so far, contrary to what I believe is a popular misconception or imagined idea of NDEs as some kinds of insubstantial and vague dreamlike visions, they are instead vastly more vivid, intense, and tangible experiences than the everyday life experience we are having right now. Our sensory inputs of seeing, hearing, etc., can be vastly more vivid. Our emotions, our sensations, and everything about our experience in the NDE world can be vastly more intense and powerful than they are here. And we can be vastly more immersed with and more in direct, tangible contact with our environment, other beings, our emotions, and even our own thoughts than we are right now. So rather than some abstract and vague imagined minor thoughts that it may be easy to carelessly imagine NDEs as, they can instead be extremely vivid, intense, and tangible experiences, vastly more vivid, intense, and tangible in every way than the experience we are having right now of daily life. That is, once again it is important to keep in mind that when we try to understand or relate to what having an NDE is phenomenologically like in these aspects, our imagination can easily do us a counterproductive disservice and lead us in the wrong and opposite direction of where we are trying to go. Therefore, as is well worth mentioning again, the difference between trying to imagine what having an NDE is phenomenologically like and understanding what having an NDE is phenomenologically like on a conceptual level should be kept in mind. However vivid, intense, or tangible we think or feel that our everyday life experience is right now, it is thus important to understand on a conceptual level that an NDE is vastly more vivid, intense, and tangible than this. As NDErs say over and over again, everything about this experience of everyday life is extremely dreamlike in comparison to what it is to be in the NDE world, including how vivid, intense, and tangible this feels or appears to be right now as we are experiencing it.

In other words, the love and the light that the NDE world seems to be made out of are things that are experienced as vastly more vivid, powerful, intense, direct, and tangible than how we experience everything right here and right now.

Furthermore, people often report a vastly expanded mind with enhanced mentation and cognition, where they have the ability to think and feel more clearly, much faster, and where they have the ability to take in and process an extraordinary amount of information immediately without a problem. Robert Perry makes a very good point about this issue:

> [O]ne of the outstanding characteristics of NDEs seems to be the intensification of all aspects of the mind. NDErs typically describe their NDE faculties of awareness, thought, feeling, sensation, and perception to be expanded in scope, intensity, and speed—to a truly incredible degree. Some NDErs report having seen with 360-degree spherical vision. Others say they instantly knew the number of hairs on a head being viewed. Others claim to have relived every second of an entire lifetime, from several perspectives at once and in exquisite detail, including what others experienced in those events—all **simultaneously**. Clearly, these descriptions indicate an almost unimaginably expanded consciousness.
>
> I can't help but think that these features contribute to the sense that what is being experienced is real. In such a state, it would seem natural to think the following: "If being in this environment means that I am **more** in every way, then that environment is itself probably more than the earthly environment—more real. And if my heightened faculties assess that environment as real, then I can probably trust those faculties even more than I trust my earthly faculties when they tell me the earthly environment is real."[106]

(emphasis in original)

Indeed, and while life reviews vary in their manifestation and the most impressive cases of life reviews are the exceptions rather than the rule when life reviews do occur in NDEs,[107] the most impressive cases of life reviews are probably the aspect of NDEs that best illustrate the coherent, rational, clear-thinking, structured, and detailed aspects of the phenomenology of an NDE. In the most impressive cases of life reviews, people are able to relive their entire life from first, second, and third person perspective respectively, simultaneously, instantly, and with perfect clarity and remembrance. The person is able to relive their own life as they first lived it from their own perspective, how everyone they ever interacted with experienced them and their actions and what they felt and thought as a result of those, and to also have an objective third person view of all that was happening. Additionally, these reviews have even been reported to include all the events of infancy and childhood that had otherwise been long forgotten.[108] And it is worth pointing out and emphasizing that when we usually remember something in our everyday life experience, it is a vague mental image that we have in our minds. But the life review in an NDE is an actual reliving with at least the same clarity, lucidity, vividness, intensity, powerfulness, directness, and tangible quality of every moment as it was actually lived when we were living our lives. In other words, this moment when I am writing these words, or when you are reading or listening to these words, will be at least as lucid, vivid, intense, powerful, direct, and tangible in a life review in an NDE as it is right now, and not as vague as the memories that you or I have right now about what you or I ate for dinner two days ago. So an experience in which one's entire life is accessible in perfect detail from numerous perspectives as clearly, lucidly, vividly, intensely, powerfully, directly, and tangibly as it was first lived for all involved, and all of it and more understood with perfect comprehension in an instant, is clearly vastly more coherent, rational, clear-thinking, structured, and detailed on every level than the experience of everyday life. Here are some illustrative comments from NDErs themselves concerning all of this:

"Nobody says that you're dying, ... you're just sort of allowed to become aware of things, and you go through a review of your past, right from when you're really tiny. You remember absolutely everything, you feel instantly all the effects of any action [you have] on another being, you just literally felt everything."[109]

"... [I] experienced a very vivid life recall. ... It was both painful and exquisitely beautiful. It was like viewing a film, filled with precise detail. Every single thought, word, deed, decision, and action was brought forth and re-experienced and re-examined. It was self-evaluation, with total transparency and honesty. Throughout, I was never judged by any of these divine beings. They simply held me in [l]ove, with complete compassion and acceptance. ... In this review, I realized that I was every single person I'd ever encountered or thought of. As I merged with and became them, I felt exactly what they experienced as a result of my loving or unloving thoughts and actions. I saw it all from their point of view, not only how my actions affected them, but then through them [how that] affected others they encountered, as the effects kept on going. ... I saw that the love we express ripples out, creating an everlasting beauty that is often unbeknownst to us at the time. ... It felt as if we are living inside a grand game, which is perfectly designed to always give us another opportunity to get it right this time. ... I saw that everything we do makes a difference. The impact we have on one another is profound. ... In this process of ruthlessly honest self-reflection, nothing went unnoticed. Nothing was able to be hidden. Nothing. Not one single thing. This life review was like going through everything with a fine-tooth comb, looking under every rock, leaving no stone unturned, seeing into each crevice with a [d]ivine [l]ight that revealed every hidden place. And through the entire process, it was all looked at and discerned through the lens of [l]ove."[110]

"[I]n a life review you see every single moment of your human life. We have total recall in our spiritual nature. Total recall. Every single moment, every single action, every single thought, word, every single sensory sensation, everything we felt from other people, it's all right there and we relive it all. It only takes a few seconds but we relive it all completely. In addition, we relive how we impacted all the other people around us. So how everyone else related to what we were saying, doing, thinking, feeling, and the ripple effect in their lives on everybody that they know."[111]

"The room seemed to be suspended in mid air, and right in the middle of the dark of space ... with swirling galaxies going on all around it. Standing on a floor that appeared as reflective, black onyx[.] ... I looked up, and saw four translucent screens begin to appear – and form a kind of gigantic, cubed box all around me. It was through this method that I was shown my life review. ... Without ever having to turn my head, I panoramically saw my past, present, future – and there was even a screen behind me that displayed a tremendous amount of scientific data, numbers, symbols and universal codes. I was in complete amazement because (as all of this was occurring) I realized I understood absolutely everything I was seeing – even in the most microscopic detail! There seemed to be no limit to the thoughts I was able to think or the ideas I was able to absorb. In this space, what we tend to think of as a limited comprehension or [single-mindedness] here on Earth, becomes truly infinite and limitless here! I kept thinking over and over how true it is what they say: that when we go back home – we all really are of [one] mind!"[112]

"The review was everything that ever happened to me, and yet it seemed to happen in just a matter of moments. And I saw it from three perspectives simultaneously. It was as though I was looking through my own eyes, experiencing it again as I first had. And then I was experiencing it through the eyes of everyone with *whom I had ever interacted. And then it was sort of, this sort of omniscient viewpoint where I can see everything. I got absolutely no judgment whatsoever. What I got was this tidal wave that hit me of this feeling of unconditional love and acceptance.*"[113]

In other words, the NDE experience seems to contain all of the coherency, rationality, clear-thinking, structure, and detail of the experience of an entire lifetime, all in a single moment. Furthermore, in that single moment there is also all of the coherency, rationality, clear-thinking, structure, and detail of every moment of what everyone else that we have ever impacted or interacted with also experienced at the same time. And all of that is at the very least, since there also seems to be a lot more going on at the same time.

Furthermore, the experience of everyday life clearly tells us that this universe has existed within itself for roughly 14.2 billion years and with a permanent structure and behavior via the fixed laws of nature, which makes the experience of participating in this level of reality a very consistent and structured experience in many ways. Every day and the experience thereof is roughly the same, and we remember a lot of everything that has happened throughout our lives and what the conditions of this level of reality are every time we wake up, and that is what helps us to conclude that the experience of everyday life is more consistent and structured and hence more real than our dreams. However, the following are the types of comments that the deepest NDErs are known to sometimes make regarding the structured, epistemic, consistent, and contextual nature of the experience of the NDE world:

"[A]nd once I realized that I saw five lights in the ... distance, and they turned out to be my five most beloved eternal friends, none of whom I'd ever known in human life. I had a life review, and during my life review I got back all the memories from hundreds

or thousands of physical lives I'd lived all over the universe. I went through a transformation process from thinking that I'm human to knowing that I'm a being of light. I got answers to all my metaphysical questions[.]"[114]

"And I went through the ceiling and I was in the atmosphere now, I was above California, and it's, I don't even know how to describe this accurately, but it kind of looked like SimCity. It didn't look real at all, like I just came from some kind of a game that was being played. Like all these little trees, and people walking around. It looked like some kind of computer game, or some simulation I was looking at. ... You know how people say that it's like a dream? Like living life is like a dream and then the other realm is the real world? I wouldn't even say that that's even a remotely accurate description. ... It was just such a minute, insignificant little experience that I had on Earth, that was just so short and temporary, that I might as well just forgotten it. ... Yeah, it was just, it was nothing. It was like 'Oh yeah, yeah he's back home' kind of a thing. And it felt like, you know how people say it feel[s] like you're home? I would go further and say that it felt more like I was there forever. It's way beyond just a feeling of being at home, that doesn't describe it very well. It's like I never left there. To be honest, I think we're all kind of there, we just, we're perceiving ourselves as being here at the moment. But we never actually completely leave that realm, I don't think we do. ... [I]t's just a short little experience, that's all. That's all life is."[115]

"[F]or me, [life is] sort of like the haunted house. When you come in, you know it's just an experience. It's small, it's just one night, right? So it's just this one life. You're eternal, you have billions of lives, so knowing that you're going to come in just for one to have an experience, though [it] may be judged as tough, or difficult, or scary, you actually chose it because you knew it was just going to be an experience, you know it's no big deal. You understand on the

other side that this part, life, is actually the dream, and you just wake up after. It's no different than one dream you had last night, out of a lifetime of dreams. This life that you're having right now is just one, it's just a blip."[116]

"I experienced being in a dark tunnel, the tunnel felt familiar[.] ... I had the feeling I had done this before. ... It seemed familiar, it seemed comfortable, it didn't seem unusual and it wasn't the least bit frightening. ... And when you're in this heavenly space you know things by thought processes, you know what each other is thinking, and it was simple and natural and wonderful. And he was beautiful, he had big blue eyes, he had a beard, a grey beard, he had a turban around his head, he was dressed in gold, and velvet, and green, and he was gorgeous, and I felt like I knew him forever. And he looked ancient and young at the same time. And he said to me, 'Are you ready to come?', it was just simple as that. And in that moment I remembered that my soul chose to come to Earth, I remembered where I was before I was born, I remembered that all of our souls choose to come here, that this is a wonderful university, that we're not here by random accident, we're not here as victims, that we come here to choose to study, to learn, and to grow. And that on some level this is like a wonderful theater, it's like a big university, we all play our part, and when our time to go comes, we leave. ... [I]n that moment you have an awakening, in that moment you often remember who you are, you remember so many things and you have access to divine knowledge and you have access to all the mysteries of the universe. ... And when you're in that light you see who you are completely, you see your flaws, you see your gifts, and you judge yourself, because everything is reflected back to you. ... [A]nd I know that we have a divine spiritual family and we are all one[.]"[117]

"It's still a very emotional thing when I talk about this because there was a point at which I could bring forth any knowledge I *wanted to have. And it was like this place was where all knowledge was."*[118]

"You just know. You're all-knowing, everything is a part of you, and it's just so beautiful. It was eternity. It's like I was always there, and I will always be there, that my existence on Earth was just a very brief instant."[119]

"Looking around at the forest I was having the experience of remembering it and knowing it was my true home, like my truest home. ... And then all at once all of this information became available to me. And I had the sensation that I already knew these answers. I already knew the information but I had completely forgotten the information while I was on Earth. ... I instantly knew I never could die and that I was eternal. But I also saw, even more powerful than that for me, because that was sort of a given for some reason in that state, 'Oh yeah, we never die, of course, you know, I forgot.' But the other part was ... I saw how innocent I really was[.] ... I was pure and I was innocent and I was deeply cherished and loved. ... The other thing I knew was that life was completely safe, my life on Earth and ... in this other realm was always safe. There was nothing ... to be afraid of ever. ... In the state I was in in my NDE I could see why. I could see ... it all come together, like ... seeing the big picture of things. ... And I saw that the place that I was in, this forest with the river and where I was, with all this knowledge, was always with me, I was never actually away from it, I just sort of thought I was all that time on Earth. ... [T]hat spiritual realm that we are a part of and from where we come from, the spiritual realm where we are truly at home, ... we're carrying it with us all the time."[120]

"And a high spiritual beingness greeted me, and there's two other spiritual beings, one on the left, one on the right. And I'm being communicated with, ... the sounds are in my mind. But I'm

greeted as an old friend and a loved brother, and that if I chose to go home, come home, I could. Yet, I had not finished what I was there to do and ... immediately the thought was communicated to me that all the skills and all the talents and everything that I've been given, which I've been very, very, very blessed with, were for a purpose. Greater than the purpose that I used to [think], the purpose of making money, and it itself wasn't it, that there was another purpose for it."[121]

"I was standing in this brilliant white light, and the light was also love or the carrier of love, and I just began to feel very blissful, very exalted. It was an incredible feeling of having been loved in a way that I didn't even know love could be, just cradled, and totally, totally, totally safe. I knew there wasn't anything that could ever harm me, nothing, I knew I could not fall into a crack in the universe and not be heard of again. I just knew that all was well, that everything was wonderful, and then there was what I always thought of as a block of knowledge, but I expect really it was a field of some kind, kind of came in and settled on me all in a piece, and I suddenly knew that I was eternal, that I was indestructible, that I had always existed, that I always would exist. I just knew that there was no end."[122]

"And what was so strange about looking at the Earth like that was that at that moment you could have asked me any given moment in my life [because] I just relived it, but you could have asked me any given moment in any person's life on that planet, and I could have told you. All that information was right there, it was available. Not just any person living there now, any person that had ever lived there or ever would live there. All that information is all available, it's right there. And what kept going through my mind at this point was, 'Of course!' I was, if you will, remembering what I had forgotten very intentionally in order to be on this planet, which is what we all do. ... [T]he truth of the matter is that we know things

when we're not here that we choose to forget while we are here. ...
[Y]ou know everything about what your life's going to be like here,
from beginning to end. You knew it before you got here, and you'll
know it again when you leave here, but while you're here you're
focused on it, and you're focused on each given moment in it. And
when you leave here, it all comes rushing back and you say, 'Of
course, yes!' ... And if you made the analogy that your life was like
a movie that you made, where you picked all of the characters and
the actors to play in your movie and you wrote the script out and
said this is what I want to have happen and how I want it to be, it
would be a very good analogy."[123]

"I started to realize that I was becoming surrounded and observed
by many beings[.] ... Every single one of these individuals was
someone I knew very well, but did not recognize as having been
a part of my life during this incarnation. Yet, the closeness and
familiarity I felt for these beloved [s]ouls surpassed any devotion for
anyone I have ever learned to [l]ove here on this planet. ... Memories
of previous, past-life experiences with these beings started [to] fill
my consciousness, and as this happened I was filled with absolute
wonder at how truly eternal we all are! I saw how life never ends[.]
... I remembered the process [of reincarnation] is endless, wonderful
and truly eternal. ... I witnessed my own spiritual evolution and
saw that I had existed long before this present incarnation (where I
am now a male human ...) For me, watching the process of living
life, after life, after life unfold, was [mind-blowing]! I undeniably
observed that I had lived an innumerable amount of lives[.] ... What
I observed ... went way beyond what I would have originally thought
'reincarnation' would be. And with reincarnation, I am not exactly
speaking about being born again and again on this planet or other
places alone. ... [My NDE] clearly showed me that these bodies (we
now inhabit) are not the first and only time we have existed! I saw
that our [s]oul and [s]pirit is ancient! I also observed that there is
no such thing as death."[124]

It is not unheard of to hear or read profound NDErs discuss how their NDE made them remember many things or sometimes even everything about eternity, or that they realized that we had always existed prior to this lifetime, or that we always will continue to exist forever after this lifetime. Some have even made comments to the effect that they remembered or realized that all of us are ultimately family, or that they remembered or realized that this life is just a preplanned and voluntary participation in a simulated existence. When we contrast these types of comments with the structured and consistent experience we all have of this world, it seems clear that the experience of the NDE world is vastly more consistent. A seemingly eternal reality that is also being remembered as such rather than merely realized as such, that has been the same way forever and that we have always been an active part of, is clearly vastly more consistent in every way than a roughly 14.2 billion-year-old universe that we have been a part of for only a few years or decades, even though our constituent parts have been with it since the beginning. And the importance of the fact that NDErs refer to it as remembering things about the afterlife can not be emphasized enough. We remember the consistency of the experience of everyday life every time we wake up from our dreams, rather than learning everything about this level of reality from scratch each and every time. Indeed, we are generally not surprised by what, where, and who we are when we wake up from a dream. In the same way, at least the deepest NDErs are known to often report that they remembered facts about the NDE level of reality rather than learned new things about a completely new place from scratch. In the deepest of NDEs it is often reported that the NDE world is very familiar, feels like home,[125] and that the beings we are closest to there are not the ones we are closest to in our earthly life, but rather those we have been friends or family with practically forever. Furthermore, the waking up process has often been reported as feeling and seeming very familiar, as many NDErs have made comments to the effect they knew that they had gone through this process many times before.

Additionally, the context in which our lives were ultimately happening starts to make a lot more sense in an NDE than it ever did when we were alive, just like the context in which our dreams are ultimately happening in makes much more sense when we wake up again back to physical life than they do when we are still dreaming. It tends to become clear to the deepest of NDErs that this life is a voluntarily chosen, relatively short experience in a role-playing scenario of a mostly fixed environment with mostly preselected character traits. In other words, from the meta-perspective of an NDE it tends to become evident that this is a simulated existence of some kind, and that participating in such a thing is a very common thing that we have done for a long time in the context of that higher reality. And just like we know not only things about our dreams but also more things about this level of reality in general when we wake up, so too do NDErs realize things not only about this reality,[126] but also gain access to more knowledge in general about that higher reality when they wake up in their NDE.

Of course, some skeptics of the survivalist interpretation of NDEs have pointed out that if NDErs truly gain access to so much knowledge in that higher reality, why do they not bring what we may consider the most important knowledge back with them, such as how to cure cancer or Alzheimer's disease, or for that matter how to build spaceships that travel as fast as possible in this universe? Disregarding how NDErs themselves might be more interested in larger, more existential questions when given such an epistemic opportunity, they also often say that they knew things in the NDE that they have since forgotten the details of. Although this certainly sounds like a convenient excuse at first to the skeptical mind, a moment's reflection makes it less so. First of all, it is very empirically possible to justifiably know that you justifiably knew something at an earlier point in time, but also that you have since forgotten it. This happens all the time in everyday life, where people study for a test, only to forget the crucial knowledge while they are taking the test. They justifiably know that they justifiably knew the information while they were still studying for the test, but have since forgotten it. But even if we disregard how this happens all the time in everyday life, there is also a larger, metacontextual reason for why this might happen to NDErs. Let us imagine for instance that it were not so, and that all NDErs came back with all the answers to absolutely everything. How fun, exciting, and immersive would this existence be if all the answers were that easy to access? There would be no inventions, discoveries, or insights through creativity, effort, and time, but all NDErs would instead just come back and write the most perfect encyclopedia ever, and all lives who could otherwise be devoted to or greatly influenced by epistemic limits would not be available in the same way to whoever it was that wanted to come here. Indeed, would living a life as a scientist or as a researcher of any kind be just as fun, exciting, or inspiring if everything were already known? How much would it not change the world from what it is now, and would it not drastically change the premortal appeal of coming here in the first place for those who want to explore what life is like with various epistemic limits? If everyday life is the simulated existence that NDErs insist that it is, then all the limitations and perceived flaws that are here are probably here intentionally to bring about the kind of unique world, society, pace of civilizational development, and personal experience that we are currently experiencing.

One final consideration regarding these three different kinds of experiences regard not so much the active phenomenology of the experience as it is happening, but how the experiences are remembered afterward. Dreams are often entirely forgotten very quickly when we wake up. Everyday life events, on the other hand, are often remembered either for life or for a while depending on how remarkable we deem them, and sometimes they are not remembered for long or even at all. But when they are remembered they are remembered as largely vague mental images and concepts. This can be clearly contrasted with how an NDE is remembered in much more vividness and detail than even everyday life events are being remembered,[127] and how the memory of an NDE usually stays completely intact over vast stretches of time.[128] Furthermore, taking the life review as an illustrative example, this entire life can be remembered even better in an NDE than it is being remembered as it is happening right now.

All of these phenomenological considerations tie back to the original reason for this lengthy elaboration. It is critically important to understand that the experience of us seemingly having brains and our brains seemingly being responsible for our mental lives at this level of reality is a phenomenological subset of everything that we experience in this everyday life level of reality. We think that we have a brain at all in the first place because of the structured and detailed nature of the experience of everyday life, which provides us with the idea of a brain in a structured form and in great detail. That is, we experience brains as having a certain shape, volume, mass, and consisting of various parts like the cerebrum, the brainstem, and the cerebellum, etc., and also as consisting of various materials like neurons, glial cells, neural stem cells, and blood vessels, etc. This is what is meant when it is said that we experience the brain as having a certain structure. Furthermore, we experience the brain as having a vast amount of neurons that are not just interacting in a very complex neuronal network, but which are also highly complex and detailed entities on their own. Additionally, the detailed nature of the experience of the brain goes even further, since as with all things it can be broken down into the core chemical or physical components and ultimately be viewed as the unfathomably complex interaction of molecules, atoms, or even elementary particles. This is what is meant by saying that our experience of the brain is a very detailed experience. Furthermore, we think that the brain is responsible for our mental lives due to the coherent and rational qualities of this everyday life level of experience, which clearly show that there is a strong correlation between mental events and brain events in a very coherent and fairly understandable and describable way. Lastly, the experience of us seemingly having brains and them being seemingly responsible for our mental lives is very consistent over vast stretches of time. From a phenomenological and ultimate viewpoint, these are the primary reasons that we actually have and use for coming to the conclusion that we and all other human beings have brains and that these brains are responsible for our mental lives at this level of experience. We can of course also see, touch, smell, hear, and in some rare cases even taste brains if we want to in order to confirm their existence, and so in that sense our experience of brains can be very vivid and tangible. We can also study and learn a lot about brains, and so in that sense our experience of brains can be a very epistemic experience. But most people who are certain of the existence of brains and their role in everyday life generally do not rely on these phenomenological qualities of their experience thereof.

When we go down a level it is clear that a similar thing is happening in our dreams. All of these qualities are greatly reduced at that level, and the experience of dreaming is therefore much less coherent, rational, structured, detailed, and consistent than the experience of everyday life. However, the experience of dreaming still manages to often fool us and make us temporarily think that we are the beings in our dreams with dream bodies and dream brains, or whatever other dream character substance and structure we may be temporarily made of therein. When we go up a level into an NDE, the vastly increased coherency, rationality, structure, detail, and consistency of the experience thereof make it even more obvious there that we are ultimately some kind of substance, essence, or mechanism in the NDE world, like a soul or a spirit, and that it is a part of that reality in an undeniable way. In other words, it is vastly more obvious in an NDE that our soul or spirit exists than it is extremely obvious to us right now that we have brains and what role they play in our everyday life, and for the very same but also vastly increased phenomenological reasons. Therefore, it becomes obvious there that the substance, essence, or mechanism in that higher reality, like a soul or a spirit, is ultimately responsible for all lower levels of experience as well, just like it is obvious at this level of everyday life that our brains are ultimately responsible for our dreams. So to argue that NDEs are likely caused by brain chemistry in light of the general coherency, rationality, structure, detail, and consistency of the experience of us seemingly having brains and of them seemingly being responsible for our mental lives in everyday life is therefore a demonstrable failure to understand, appreciate, and accept what having an NDE is phenomenologically like on a conceptual level. Of course, it is and always will remain logically possible that NDEs are actually caused by brain chemistry anyway somehow,[129] but a clear understanding of what having an NDE is phenomenologically like on a conceptual level should lead us to the understanding that it is extremely unlikely that NDEs are actually caused by brain chemistry. Indeed, it is just as unlikely, if not more so, as the possibility that our experience of everyday life right now is actually and ultimately caused by the brain chemistry of our dream characters. That too is and always will remain a logical possibility that a very small minority of philosophers may continue to worry and write about for a long time to come, but no one treats it as a practical, empirical, or remotely likely possibility that we should actually take seriously, and justifiably so. Similarly, to the extent that we are able to understand, appreciate, and accept what having an

NDE is phenomenologically like on a conceptual level, it should increasingly become as obvious to us from a rational point of view as it already is to NDErs from an experiential point of view that it is extremely unlikely that NDEs are caused by the brain chemistry of our here and now level of reality characters.

This is also why it should not come as a surprise at all to anyone who understands this line of reasoning that even those who are the most familiar with or persuaded by the neurophysiological argument are completely unable to resist the force of the realer than real argument once properly experienced firsthand. A good way to illustrate this more concretely is to imagine that you have a dream one night that you are a person who has great knowledge and practical experience with brains and how their activity impacts cognition. Say that you dream that you are a neuroscientist, a neurosurgeon, or a philosopher of mind. In either scenario you are a professional who is acutely aware of all the various ways in which the activity in the brain correlates to mental events and abilities. So, say for instance that you have a dream about being a neurosurgeon. In the dream you are not just aware of all of the vast literature and the endless articles and books that clearly demonstrate the exceedingly intimate relationship between mental events and brain events, but you also routinely do experiments on volunteers, and see firsthand how your experiments impact their cognition and their cognitive abilities. Additionally, your colleagues do similar experiments on you that you voluntarily participate in, and you get to experience while in the dream how your cognition and cognitive abilities change as a result of what they do. While in this dream, you have every single reason to think that everything that you experience is a direct consequence of what is happening to and in your dream character brain.

Now, after a while you wake up from this dream back to daily life. Would it make sense to conclude, then, that you are still that neurosurgeon having an ultrareal experience of what we call daily life as a result of some experiment, drug intake, or some abnormal brain state being reached in that dream? Or would it make more sense that you are a person who had a dream one night about being a neurosurgeon, and that daily life is not just some seemingly ultrareal hallucination from the perspective of the dream world but is rather a more primary reality altogether? The literature on the relationship between mental events and brain events while in the context of being a neurosurgeon in the dream may seem impressive, and the experience of the dream character brains may seem vivid and tangible as you work with them and touch them routinely while in the dream, but it still seems deeply obvious that the latter is the vastly more reasonable conclusion. It should come as absolutely no surprise at all, then, that when a former Harvard neurosurgeon who was a materialist prior to his NDE actually had an NDE of the deeper variety and experienced the ultrareality of the NDE world, that was enough to thoroughly convince him beyond any rational doubt that the NDE world was the primary reality.[130] No matter how impressed or swayed someone may feel or be by the neurophysiological argument, by how closely interwoven brain activity and mental activity seem to be in everyday life, it will always boil down to the fact that they are essentially impressed or swayed by the level of phenomenological coherency, rationality, structure, detail, epistemic quality, and consistency of the experience of everyday life, or specifically of the subset experience of people seemingly having brains. When skeptics of the survivalist interpretation of the NDE appeal to how the brain is built with all the various areas of the brain being responsible for different things, they are essentially appealing to how phenomenologically structured our everyday life subset experience of the brain is. When they appeal to all the various neurotransmitters and their network, or to how complex the brain is at a cellular, molecular, atomic, or elementary particle level, they are essentially appealing to how phenomenologically detailed our everyday life subset experience of the brain is. When they appeal to how much neuroscientists have learned about the brain and how it works, they are essentially appealing to how phenomenologically epistemic our everyday life subset experience of the brain is. When they appeal to the impressive correlations between mental states and brain states, they are essentially appealing to how phenomenologically coherent and rational our everyday life subset experience of the brain is. When they appeal to how all of this seems to remain true over vast amounts of time, how our brains existed and functioned in the same way in the past, how our brains exist and function the same way right now, and how our brains in all likelihood will continue to exist and function in the same way in the future, they are essentially appealing to how phenomenologically consistent our everyday life subset experience of the brain is. And so on.

When we are impressed or swayed by the neurophysiological argument we are essentially impressed or swayed by a specific degree of a consistent pattern at this everyday life level of experience. And since the experience of an NDE is known to be vastly more impressive than the experience of everyday life in all phenomenological aspects, the vastly enhanced degree of the consistent pattern of the higher reality is vastly more impressive and justifiably convincing in all ways. Therefore, neither the neurophysiological argument nor materialism as a whole have any rational relevance or sway left for the sufficiently deep NDEr, or for the person who thoroughly understands the phenomenology of an NDE on a conceptual level and the philosophical gravity thereof.

While so far at least we have not found any consistent correlations between NDEs and things happening in the brain,[131] we could pretend for the sake of argument that there were such findings available. Indeed, let us imagine the idea of being able to push a button, which would in turn reliably alter our brain chemistry, which would in turn reliably produce a profound NDE. And let us imagine that we could then carefully observe how our brain chemistry was being altered and how the activity in the brain behaved as this was happening. Let us say that our memory circuits were demonstrably lit up as we were having a life review, or that our endorphins were overflowing as we were feeling the bliss in an NDE, etc. All areas of the brain that have been speculated by some scientists to be correlated with the NDE were lit up. Or better yet, the entire brain became maximally active in all areas, so that no one could deny that a lot of things were demonstrably and reliably happening in the brain when people had profound NDEs.

When a person came back from such an experience and were shown the brain scans and the activity of their brain while they were having a profound NDE, however, they would still be completely justified for thinking that the NDE was indicative of a higher reality for all of the phenomenological considerations that have been elaborated upon herein. If this still sounds even slightly unreasonable to anyone then we just compare the issue with dreams one more time. Let us say that we were in a dream with a team of neuroscientists and neurosurgeons, and we had a button that made us have the experience of waking up into real life for five minutes, and then we fell back asleep again. When we returned to the team of neuroscientists and neurosurgeons in the dream, they would show us how we were catapulted into the experience of waking life as a result of them pressing a button, and they could show us all about the events that happened in our dream character brains while we were having that experience, and how certain areas of our dream character brain started to operate slightly differently. But in that dream, while having perpetual access to the perfect memory of what it was phenomenologically like to wake up for five minutes, we all know that it would not matter at all what correlations between our dream character brain and our experience of waking life was like that was provided by those dream neuroscientists and dream neurosurgeons. This is because those correlations would be appeals to the level of phenomenological coherency, rationality, structure, detail, epistemic quality, and consistency of the dream experience, and we had just experienced all of those phenomenological aspects in a vastly enhanced manner in our experience of waking life. And the same is true for whatever correlations we may find in the brain and the NDE at this everyday life level of experience. No matter how impressed someone may be by those at this level of reality, they will just be appealing to the level of phenomenological coherency, rationality, structure, detail, epistemic quality, and consistency of the everyday life subset experience of people seemingly having brains. And since the NDEr has experienced all of those phenomenological qualities in a vastly enhanced manner they will not impress the NDEr in the slightest, just like we would not be impressed by the same thing happening in our dreams if we could remember with crystal clarity what it was phenomenologically like to experience everyday life while we were still dreaming. And this is precisely why it does not even matter whether we will ever find a way to reliably induce a profound NDE or not, regardless of whether it is through the use of psychoactive drugs, electrical brain stimulation, or some other way, and why it also does not even matter whether we will ever find and demonstrate correlations between the NDE and activity in the brain. The person who has experienced a profound NDE will always be forced to choose between trusting the experience of the consistent pattern that this level of experience provides, and the experience of the vastly more impressive consistent pattern that the NDE world provided. And there will never be a reason to trust in the experience of the vastly less impressive consistent pattern. In other words and to summarize, everyday life is ultimately just an experience of a consistent pattern, and an NDE is an experience of a far more consistent and far more impressive, coherent, rational, structured, detailed, and epistemic pattern. So potential future findings of correlations between NDEs and brain events will for all of these reasons never be a relevant counterargument to the self-evident reality of NDEs to NDErs, or to those who understand the phenomenology of the NDE on a conceptual level and the epistemic relevance thereof.

While less of a phenomenological issue and more of a practical concern, the difference in emotional, technological, and overall civilizational maturity between the experiences must also be strikingly relevant to the NDErs' judgment of its realness. If the NDE world is an eternal dimension of divine perfection as reported by many NDErs, then it is not a stretch to argue that it is also extremely if not infinitely or maximally evolved and advanced in all areas of knowledge, wisdom, inquiry, or development imaginable. To illustrate the gravity of this insight by analogy, imagine that even if humanity has a tremendously positive development arc into a utopian society in the ultradeep future, billions of years and beyond from now, where we will be way more advanced in every single way than we can even imagine it to be possible right now, the NDE world would probably still be vastly more evolved, advanced, and developed than even that. Indeed, billions of years of civilizational development can never compare to an eternity of the same having already transpired in the NDE world, unless of course the ceiling for civilizational advancement and development turns out to be relatively low in all areas. The important implication of this is that waking up in the NDE world is at least as impressive as it would be to take a time machine and travel to the peak of human civilization, however far away in the future it may lie, and stay there for days, weeks, months, years, or even decades, and then come back to the present day. While arriving in the utopian society in the ultradeep future must surely be a tremendous culture shock, you would eventually get quite used to it. But just like arriving in such a future must be a culture shock at first, so too must it be to come back to the present day once a person has gotten used to the vastly more impressive alternative. And of course, waking up in the NDE world and coming back to this world afterward are events that are more of a culture shock than any time travel back and forth in this universe ever could be.

When we are talking about things that differ between our current society and the ultradeep future, this includes not just things like technology, societal structure, or space travel milestones, which are things that we tend to consider the most indicative of civilizational progress here and now. But it is worth noting that many skeptics of the survivalist interpretation of NDEs seem to think along the lines of, "We are learning more and more about this particular universe, we are learning more and more about how it works and why, and we are learning more and more about what we can do with that knowledge. Therefore, this particular universe is in all probability all that exists." This self-evidently does not follow, of course, but it still seems to be persuasive on a psychological level to many people who are amazed by the scientific and technological progress and the pace thereof of our civilization these last few decades or centuries. It is as if the notion that the NDE world has vastly more advanced technology than ours has not even entered their minds as a serious possibility, and they hold on to the idea that a higher reality that does not share the same or similar parameters as this particular universe must be as technologically primitive and ignorant as the imagined notions thereof of people in the Middle Ages and antiquity would have us all believe. But more than differences with respect to technology, societal structure, or space travel milestones, the differences between our phase of civilizational development and the ultradeep future also include things like attitude, morality, ethics, values, or how to best relate to existence in general, or how to be as virtuous beings as possible, or how to be the best ourselves we possibly can be, or how to live as ideal as possible. This challenging and imperfect physical world, our egoistically inclined human minds, and this demonstrably pre-utopian society and phase of civilizational development often tempts and incentivizes us to be less kind, loving, accepting, forgiving, caring, compassionate, sympathetic, humble, honest, genuine, appreciative, fun-loving, self-improving, etc., than we possibly can be. However, the NDE world tends to provide a stark contrast to this with an emotional maturity permeating not just the beings encountered therein, but also that entire plane of existence. It is, after all, a documented fact that NDErs often come back and do not just have a problem integrating the experience for what it was and what it implied, but also have a problem with being the same people they were before, and with maintaining the same values and the same approach to life and other people.

Of course, it is often easier and pragmatically advantageous to just internalize and accept the contemporary value systems and groupthink of the culture we find ourselves in when growing up in a society, rather than disregard all that dogma and just pursue what we consider to be our ideal personal development as if we lived in a cultural vacuum. This is because peer exclusion, bullying, and ridicule are often undesirable consequences for going our own way and forging our own value system in light of reason rather than cultural dogma, and these consequences are not easy things to handle for most people. This is just as true for NDErs as for the rest of us, but NDErs often do not always have much of a choice. Once someone has seen, felt, and experienced how awesome existence could be if we all, metaphorically speaking, grew up and become more emotionally mature, responsible, and serious, instead of just being unreflectively accepting of the normalized emotional immaturity that this world, society, and even our own minds expect of us, it must surely be hard to take the entire experience of this world seriously after that. Our current phase of civilizational development, despite being much more advanced and civilized than our past, is still in all likelihood prehistoric relative to what any beings living in the ultradeep future will come to think about us. So waking up into an NDE must not just be like waking up from any random dream, but like waking up from a dream about being an unenlightened hunter-gatherer living in the Stone Age, having had a deeply primitive value system and approach to life while in the dream. So coming back to this world after having had an NDE and noticing how people think, behave, and what they value and put the most emphasis on must quite literally be a very caveman-esque kind of bizarre experience.

And it may be worth pointing out and emphasizing that NDErs are for all of the elaborated upon reasons and considerations in this chapter vastly more justifiably certain and convinced that they experienced the real world than the protagonist Neo from the movie *The Matrix* ever was or could have been justifiably certain and convinced that he just had woken up from the Matrix and into the real world. But even if the NDE was only just as real as the experience of this life, would it still not make more sense to trust in the NDE for the aforementioned reason and consideration alone? In other words, when people woke up in a world or a reality that was in the future relative to us, and thus woke up in a reality that therefore was more evolved and technologically advanced, would it not make more sense to trust in that reality even if all other things were equal, and the experience was not more real than real in other ways as it is with NDEs? This is basically what happens in the movie *The Matrix*, where the protagonist Neo wakes up in the near future, only somewhere around 200 years ahead of his timeline in the simulated reality. There he is shown a lot more technology, including the technology that can make the sort of simulations that he just came from transpire (so it is admittedly also a more contextual experience for Neo). Why should it make more sense to trust in a place that is a chaotic world filled with technological, physical, and cognitive limits, irrationality, evil, childish behavior, widespread emotional immaturity, egoistical and counter-productive values, tremendous inefficiency on all levels, a noticeable lack of social and environmental harmony, etc., rather than a reality that is more impressive than we can even imagine the ultradeep future to be, and which is clearly extremely if not maximally advanced and evolved in every conceivable area of development?

Indeed, imagine that one is presented with an experience of two different realities, and one of them has the ability and technology to provide us with a custom-designed simulated experience, and they say and demonstrate that this is what is happening and why we have the experience of the other reality. In the experience of the other reality, they do not have this ability or this technology, or at least not yet. In this scenario, how is it not more reasonable to trust in the experience of the reality that has that ability and that technology, if all other things are equal? It is of course not necessitated by this difference, but it must surely be a reasonable and relevant consideration when trying to figure out which reality caused the other.

All of this also ties into the discussion about the difference in seriousness and purposefulness between the experiences. Many non-NDErs seem to dismiss NDEs because they are so filled with positive emotions, as if they are therefore too good to be true, or they sound too much like something that supposedly unserious hippies or generally goofy people would say, with all the talk about love, peace, and acceptance, etc. In my estimation, however, many who think that the NDE world sounds too good to be true seem to suffer from some kind of existential Stockholm syndrome, where the limited, challenging, and sometimes horrible nature of this particular reality has been deeply internalized as some kind of universal default, requirement, or necessity. This seems to make them think that all worlds or levels of reality must be at least as limited, challenging, or horrible as this world or level of reality, or at least close to it in these aspects, before they can think of them as serious possibilities that could really exist. The materialization of this mindset is often found in sayings such as, "You need bad times in order to appreciate good times." But this is of course nothing more than an existential coping mechanism. Instead of just accepting that this particular reality can be and often is more horrible than objectively necessary and leaving it at that, many people needlessly infer the generalization from that that it must therefore apply to all conceivable realities.

In other words, due to how wonderful the NDE world sounds, a fair amount of non-NDErs seem to think that NDEs are therefore not only not very serious experiences, but go even further and think of them as very non-serious experiences that can be laughingly dismissed as self-evident hallucinatory nonsense. But what could possibly be more existentially serious and purposeful than figuring out what the best possible emotions are, and then trying our best to sustain them as much as possible? What could be more serious and purposeful than developing an as emotionally productive, healthy, and harmonious attitude to existence as possible? Are our feelings ultimately not the most important things in our lives? To feel good, to feel peaceful, to feel acceptance, to feel love, and to feel happy. What could possibly be more important, and hence more serious and purposeful, than that? All other things we do in life are usually just means to achieve such an end. We take seriously our own and others' work, health, safety, etc., so that we can all have better means to sustain our material existence, so that we can in turn do more of the things that make us feel good things over a sustainable long-term period. Even when we dedicate ourselves to helping others or humanity as a whole in various ways, we do it so that we can feel good about ourselves, and feel love, kindness, self-realization, generosity, achievement, purpose, or contentment. When we are talking about being serious and having purpose, we are talking about things that actually matter, and about which things that matter the most. Why would the most enlightened and self-realized beings not want to feel as much of the best positive emotions at all times as possible? And hence, why would a higher reality not have their entire reality overflowing with such emotions to the extent that they are capable of achieving it? Is it really that speculative to think that the NDE world is overflowing with practically infinite unconditional love, acceptance, peace, and bliss because those are what was long ago realized as the best feelings that provide the most enjoyment and purpose out of existence? Indeed, would the NDE be a more serious experience if it were accompanied by a feeling of pure neutrality and involved no emotions whatsoever, and instead of finding themselves in gorgeous and alive landscapes where everyone and everything was sparkling, singing, or dancing, the NDErs found themselves in lackluster office environments? Of course, feeling too much happiness or love while we are at work as humans would arguably distract us from our ability to focus and do the work that we must do to keep society running. But our inability to multitask these things is not an argument for why other realities must share such frustrating limitations, and if we could multitask the feeling of intense love and bliss with working, would it not be a much more existentially serious choice to do so, and would we not feel a lot more purpose and meaning in our lives?

NDErs are for all of these aforementioned reasons and considerations often a lot more justifiably certain that they experienced a more real reality than this one during their NDE than they are about anything else in this world. Therefore, it follows that they are even more epistemically justified in claiming that the afterlife is real based on their experience of it than the people who have visited the room are for having observed and verified the existence of the shining pink elephant, or anything else in that room. Not only was the NDE experienced as vastly more vivid, intense, and tangible, etc., than the experience of the room, but the NDE is also remembered afterward with crystal clarity, whereas the memory of being inside of the room would presumably fade away and become very vague in much the same way that most of our memories fade away and become very vague. Indeed, NDErs are for these aforementioned reasons and considerations not just more justifiably certain about the reality of an afterlife than the people who have been inside of the room are justifiably certain about whatever they have experienced and confirmed the existence of in the room, but NDErs are also more justifiably certain about the existence of an afterlife than any scientist has ever been justifiably certain of anything when it comes to how this world works. After all, both scientists and those who have been inside of the room are still certain about details in the context of this reality and the general pattern of behavior it seems to follow, and being certain about things in this reality is to first be certain about this reality. Since NDErs are insisting that the justified certainty of the existence of the NDE world is even more firm and obvious to them than the justified certainty we all have about the existence of this world, and since testimonies transmit not just knowledge but also the justification for that knowledge,[132] we can therefore be even more justifiably certain about the reality of an afterlife than we can be about whatever is reported to be found in such a room.

Chapter 5

Muddying The Waters

The aforementioned scenario regarding the room and the shining pink elephant is presenting a slightly simplified picture for illustrative purposes. When it comes to NDEs as they are currently defined and their depth categorized, the situation is a bit more complicated than the one-dimensional scenario of absolutely everyone agreeing with each other vehemently on the issue of survival. I felt that it was best to describe the argument in its simplest and purest form before going into detail about how the data is not as clear-cut as it would be if all NDErs were certain of the existence of an afterlife and if all NDEs were reported as more real than real. While this was an overgeneralization, it essentially does apply to a definable subset of all NDErs, the details and relevance of which will be elaborated upon and made clear in this chapter of the book.

The thought experiment that was created and introduced in the third chapter of this book was presented at first in its strongest possible form to thoroughly demonstrate and emphasize its epistemic force, but it actually comes in at least five possible and generalized scenarios:

1. People who go into the room have the time and the tools to thoroughly investigate the inside of the room.
2. People who go into the room have a lot less time but still have tools with which to investigate the inside of the room.
3. People who go into the room have the time but not any tools with which to investigate the inside of the room.
4. People who go into the room have neither much time nor any tools with which to investigate the inside of the room.

5. It is randomly selected which of the four previous scenarios the person entering the room gets to have.

At least on first reflection, clearly the first scenario is the most impressive where both we and the randomly selected people going in there can be the most confident in what is really in there, and clearly the fourth scenario is the least impressive where both we and the randomly selected people experiencing it can have the least confidence in what is really in there. Furthermore, since a definable subset of those entering the room in the fifth scenario do so under the conditions of the first scenario, it seems clear that the fifth scenario is more impressive than both the second and the third scenarios, albeit maybe not necessarily at a very low number of randomly selected people going through these various scenarios. However, once we have thousands or more of randomly selected people going through either scenario, and the distribution between the various scenarios that those in the fifth scenario enter is fairly evenly distributed, then the fifth scenario is at least as impressive as the first scenario at roughly one lower magnitude of randomly selected people entering the room. Lastly, it is arguably up for further discussion which of the second and the third scenarios gives both us and the randomly selected people entering the room the most justified confidence about what is in there. Indeed, the answer may even vary and be contingent on what particular thing is being reported to be found in that room, and therefore it is best left an open question at this point.

NDErs as a whole are figuratively and roughly finding themselves in the fifth scenario, albeit the fact that the distribution between the four generalized scenarios that they get to figuratively experience may not be evenly distributed with twenty-five percent of NDErs for each. Of course, the first four scenarios could and arguably should be subdivided even further to properly accommodate the variety of depth an

NDE can have, but this categorization is sufficient for present purposes to illustrate the general point of how NDEs as a whole relate to the room analogy. For these reasons it is therefore relevant to go into more detail about what all of this entails in this chapter of the book.

But a few comments about the fifth scenario are in order, because in some ways it is more impressive than the first scenario, at least when it comes to the room analogy, and at least when the amount of randomly selected people who get to enter are in the thousands or tens of thousands and beyond. If someone wants to bribe, threaten, or bribe and threaten the randomly selected people who enter the room, they would have much more time to really convince everyone to comply in the first scenario than in the fifth, since it could be quite difficult to convincingly bribe, threaten, or bribe and threaten everyone in just a few minutes, or even just a few seconds. And of course, the idea that all the randomly selected people could learn or be taught how to lie convincingly in such a short time period is beyond wildly unreasonable. Furthermore, some might want to argue for the logical possibility that when randomly selected people enter the room they just find an operating room, where they have their brains operated on and perfectly reprogrammed to believe that there is a brown table with a white plate on it in the room, or a shining pink elephant, or that the laws of physics are being violated in there, or whatever else. This is of course currently not even remotely possible with modern technology and would require ultra-advanced futuristic technology or alien technology, if it is even empirically possible altogether for ultra-advanced civilizations to do this in this particular universe. But it gets even crazier when you take the fifth scenario into account. They would essentially need to be able to laserbeam a perfect reprogramming of everyone's brain in the matter of a few seconds, all the while leaving zero traces of having actually done so on the person, neither physically nor mentally, so that the experience of entering the room, being inside of it and investigating it, and exiting it feels like a perfectly consistent, normal, and continuous experience for all people with different brain chemistry. And how is that not more extraordinary than whatever else that might actually be reported to exist in there? It is another one of those logical possibilities of course, but we have absolutely no reason to believe that it is anything other than a beyond astronomically unlikely logical possibility. And indeed, just like how the argument that the randomly selected people entering the room are bribed, threatened, or bribed and threatened in the room could also apply to scientists in the real world, so too the logical possibility exists that very rich people or for that matter aliens are perfectly reprogramming the brains of scientists and journal editorial teams from afar in the real world. But what rational person discredits scientific findings because of that ever-present logical possibility? Furthermore, some might want to argue that the idea that the laws of physics are being violated in the room is more extraordinary than instant and perfect laserbeam reprogramming of everyone's brains, so that we should therefore always prefer to believe in the latter if the randomly selected people coming out of the room claimed the former. However, then they have essentially made the laws of physics unfalsifiable, because it is just as logically possible that very rich people or aliens are perfectly reprogramming the brains of scientists, journal editorial teams, and everyone who tries to look at the supposed evidence from afar with laserbeams in the real world as the idea that they would do so in that room. Indeed, if scientists ever do discover evidence that the laws of physics are being violated in the real world, would it therefore be more reasonable to believe that very rich people or aliens are perfectly reprogramming their brains from afar, just because it is logically possible and sounds less extraordinary to us? So whatever counterargument to the room analogy someone might want to try to weave together, to argue for something that possibly might exist or happen in the room that better explains what everyone reports, it has to be actually likely and not just a logical possibility, and it also has to account for why the same reasoning should not also affect our reasons for believing in scientists in general in the real world.

As a brief aside before moving on, it should also be mentioned that comparing NDEs and all the facts surrounding them and the variability in the reports to a single room is overly simplistic, and that a more proper way of doing it would be to have the figurative scenario be a very large, equally well-protected house with many different rooms in it. This way, visitors to the house would have the time to explore some of the rooms within it, but not all of them, and that is what we find in the NDE data as well since very few (if any) NDErs experience everything that can be experienced in an NDE in their own NDE. This would more aptly accommodate the commonalities but also the variability between NDE reports, and account for why not all people experience the exact same thing in there. However, since this book only concerns itself with the issue of whether there is an afterlife or not, and largely ignores the issues of the nature, structure, content, value system, etc., of the afterlife, a single room with a single object in it is enough for this relatively simple purpose. A more accurate figurative scenario of NDEs would be to have a very large well-protected house with many rooms in it, but with a shining pink elephant in the entrance hall that can be observed and investigated as soon as a person enters the house. The room or the house represents the NDE in either scenario, and the actual existence of the shining pink elephant in the room or the entrance hall of the house represents the actual existence of an afterlife that is being justifiably realized as factual for the NDEr. I would therefore enthusiastically encourage more ambitious writers than me to expand on this improved analogy as a conceptual approach to have justified understanding about what we can possibly know with some degree of certainty about the nature, structure, content, value system, etc., of the afterlife. After all, we can know facts and details about the nature, structure, content, value system, etc., of the afterlife that NDErs are reporting about for the very same reason that we can know facts and details about what would be in the various rooms of such a building.

At this stage, I think it is necessary to go into more detail about the fact that there are different depths to NDEs. As research began more seriously on the NDE in the late 1970s it became evident that some kind of tool was necessary to determine whether someone had had an NDE and to measure the depth of the NDE. The first attempt at this was the Weighted Core Experience Index,[133] which was later criticized and argued to be improved upon by the NDE Scale (or the Greyson Scale).[134] The NDE Scale, for instance, asks the individual whether they have had, and to which degree, some of the sixteen elements most indicative of having had an NDE. This is how leading NDE researcher Sam Parnia summarizes how this works:

The Greyson Scale gives each of the 16 features a score of 0, 1, or 2. The score depends first on whether the feature has been experienced, and second on how intense the experience has been. Therefore, using this scale, anyone's experience can be graded and given a score. There's a potential maximum score of 32, but for an experience to be defined as an NDE, Greyson stated that a minimum score of 7 was needed.

Since the early 1980s, research studies have used one of these two scales to standardize and compare the NDE experiences recounted by people. Although both research scales have some limitations in their day-to-day applications, they've been particularly useful during research because they've provided a basic means of defining an NDE and semi-quantifying the depth of the experience.[135]

So for instance on the NDE Scale, those who score 0-6 are

regarded as having had no NDEs, while those who score 7-14 are regarded as having had NDEs for research purposes, albeit subtle ones. Those who score 15-23 are regarded as having had deep NDEs, and those with scores between 24-32 are regarded as having had profound NDEs. This categorization of the depth of an NDE is defined by how far away from the standard deviation of an average NDE they are.[136]

As previously noted, the aftereffect of certainty in survival and an afterlife is strongly correlated with the increased depth of the experience, and when it comes to those who have had profound NDEs and the deepest of NDEs in general, they seemingly always come back certain of or at least believing in an afterlife based on their experience.[137] While there has been until recently a general neglect in the study of the difference in aftereffects between subtle, deep, and profound NDErs, including their belief in survival and an afterlife, it still remains the case that as far as I and other NDE researchers I have corresponded with are aware of after going through thousands of NDEs including hundreds of profound NDEs, there are either no exceptions in the literature, or they must be exceedingly rare.[i]

There are, however, many exceptions when it comes to those who have had subtle NDEs, and at least some exceptions when it comes to those who have had deep NDEs. Furthermore, a positive NDE is not the only thing that can happen when a person comes close to death, as there are also those who have hellish NDEs, those who have an insufficient amount of NDE elements to have their experience classified as an NDE, and those who have no experience whatsoever or minor non-NDE like hallucinations. When a person has a survived proximity to death, there are essentially five different generalized scenarios that can unfold in terms of how that category of experience may or may not come to change that person's stance on whether there exists an afterlife or not:

1. Hellish NDE.[138]
2. No experience whatsoever or minor non-NDE like hallucinations.[139]
3. No NDE, i.e., a 0-6 score on the NDE Scale.
4. Subtle or deep NDE, where it is not sufficiently deep to convince a person of the existence of an afterlife.
5. Profound NDE, or a deep or subtle NDE that is sufficiently deep to convince a person of the existence of an afterlife.

Regarding hellish NDEs, these can manifest in three different ways. Either they are classically horrendous with a person experiencing demons or other hellish scenarios, or they are of an endless dark void where the person feels that nothing exists whatsoever, or even that nothing has ever existed and that their entire life was a lie. The third manifestation of a hellish NDE is where they are like the initial stages of the ordinary, blissful NDEs, but are perceived negatively. For instance, someone may be deeply uncomfortable with letting go of their earthly life, and being sucked into the tunnel or leaving the body can be very discomforting experiences. While the experience of a meaningless void usually does not turn into a blissful NDE, the other two kinds of hellish NDEs more often than not turn into blissful NDEs eventually as the experience goes on, but not always. Although this could be due to the duration of the hellish NDE being too short, just like how ordinary NDEs vary in depth and duration, this remains speculative at this point. Either way, people who have hellish NDEs are in general about as certain of survival as ordinary NDErs,[140] but more research on hellish NDEs is definitely needed.

Most people who come close to death have no experience whatsoever during this event, and a minority have some minor non-NDE like hallucinations that are realized as hallucinations to the person who has them. This scenario has nowhere near as dramatic effects, on average, on a person's belief regarding the existence of an afterlife as either the scenario of having an NDE Scale score of 0-6, or the scenarios of having various types of NDEs.[141] The fact that most people who come close to death do not report an NDE may be argued by some to be indicative of them getting a look at what death is and observing that it is the nothingness that physicalism predicts, and that the majority of people are hence supposedly in disagreement with NDErs on what death entails. However, this interpretation is falsified when it is realized that some people have come close to death multiple times, yet have had NDEs some of those times but not all of them.[142] Since people can come close to death and not have any experience during that episode, only to later change their mind on the issue of survival after an NDE accompanied their subsequent proximity to death,[143] it becomes clear that having an NDE or not and how it is interpreted is the defining aspect of this discussion, not whether someone was close to death or not. From the perspective of the room analogy, I think it is therefore reasonable and fair to view all people who come close to death as people who got to the building in which the room is situated (at the very best, if they are not an irrelevant cohort altogether), but only those who had an NDE as those who actually were allowed to go into the room.

Then there are those who score 0-6 on the NDE Scale and hence have no NDEs but also are not part of the category of people who have no experience whatsoever during their proximity to death. The existence of this cohort of people could perhaps be argued to highlight how the definition and categorization of NDEs is a bit like the sorites paradox, and that researchers are forced to draw a line somewhere. Not too surprisingly, these people have on average an increased belief in the existence of an afterlife, but less so than NDErs.[144]

When it comes to the small minority of people who are unconvinced of the existence of an afterlife after their subtle or even deep NDE, this might be invoked by some as an argument against the room analogy, since not everyone who went in there became thoroughly convinced of the existence of the shining pink elephant if the room analogy is meant to mirror the NDE situation of our world. However, I find that to be a hasty conclusion, and wish to suggest that the depth of the NDE is a rough approximation for how long a time a person is given to inspect the room in the analogy. If someone is only given a few minutes to inspect the room, can we really expect them to rule out all possible ways in which the shining pink elephant might be an optical illusion of some kind? Some people may not be comfortable with rushing to conclusions, and while they might see and touch the elephant, and understand why others arrive at the conclusion that it is there and real, they still might feel that they were not given a proper chance to truly investigate the matter and be comfortably certain. Those who got to stay in the room for hours or days, on the other hand, would have a lot more time to get a good look and investigate the matter thoroughly, and hence their view on the matter would be a lot more relevant, given that their epistemic justification for their conclusion is a lot more solid than those who only got a quick visit of the room.

Finally there is the matter that not all NDErs describe their NDE as more real than real, but the situation is very similar here as with the aftereffect of being certain of survival. As the NDE becomes deeper, the quality of the experience to be more real than this life is a lot more likely to be present.[145] This seems to be very consistent with a survivalist interpretation of the phenomenon, as the closer to and more integrated with the supposed afterlife the experiencer becomes the more self-evident it becomes to them that it actually is the afterlife. This observation also helps to explain and illuminate why there are no known exceptions to profound NDErs with a belief or certainty in the existence of an afterlife in the whole NDE literature. To tie this fact together with the room analogy, it could be argued that those who experienced the heightened realness were those that were allowed to bring with them the additional equipment to investigate whatever they were to find in the room, and those who did not experience the heightened realness were allowed to go in there and look, but not take anything with them into the room whatsoever.

We have a figurative epistemic scenario where a small minority of millions or tens of millions of people who are representative of the population as a whole who come out of the room do not deny that it appears as if there was a shining pink elephant in the room, but remain uncertain as to what to believe about whether it was really there or not.[ii] While this might be an initial cause for some skepticism, the picture changes when it is revealed that the only reason that they were not able to make a judgment call about whether the shining pink elephant was truly there or not, or lean towards skepticism, is that they feel that they did not get the chance to investigate the matter thoroughly and only got a quick visit of the room, and usually without the aid of any equipment. All in all the overwhelming majority, including everyone who has actually gotten the time to investigate it thoroughly and with equipment, are certain that there is a shining pink elephant in the room. The only ones who have any reservation about it are a minority of those that only got to investigate the room for a sometimes short but more often very short amount of time, and usually did so without the aid of any equipment, and thus could not be expected to make as thorough an investigation of the room as they might prefer, yet still concede that it at least appears as if there is a shining pink elephant in the room. In light of these considerations, is it not fairly obvious still that it is beyond astronomically likely that there is a shining pink elephant in the room?

i. For instance, NDE researcher Jeffrey Long analyzed 596 of his most recently received NDE testimonies of people who had an NDE Scale score of at least 7, who only had one NDE, and who shared their NDE in English, and found that 48 of them had an NDE Scale score of 25-32. When this cohort of people were asked about their attitude to the existence of an afterlife prior to their NDE, out of five possible answers to the question 14 responded, "An afterlife definitely exists"; 9 responded, "An afterlife probably exists"; 14 responded, "I was uncertain if an afterlife exists"; 4 responded, "An afterlife probably does not exist"; 2 responded, "An afterlife does not exist"; and 5 did not answer about their belief in an afterlife prior to their experience. All 48, however, responded that at the current time they believe that "An afterlife definitely exists" (Long, 2018).

ii. There were 251 respondents with subtle NDEs with an NDE Scale score of 7-14 in Long's sample. When this cohort of people were asked about their attitude to the existence of an afterlife prior to their subtle NDE, out of five possible answers to the question 67 responded, "An afterlife definitely exists"; 51 responded, "An afterlife probably exists"; 72 responded, "I was uncertain if an afterlife exists"; 18 responded, "An afterlife probably does not exist"; 17 responded, "An afterlife does not exist"; and 26 did not answer about their belief in an afterlife prior to their experience. After their subtle NDE, 195 responded, "An afterlife definitely exists"; 31 responded, "An afterlife probably exists"; 18 responded, "I am uncertain if an afterlife exists"; 3 responded, "An afterlife probably does not exist"; 1 responded, "An afterlife does not exist"; and 3 did not give an answer. There were 297 respondents with deep NDEs with an NDE Scale score of 15-24 in Long's sample. When this cohort of people were asked about their attitude to the existence of an afterlife prior to their deep NDE, out of five possible answers to the question 68 responded, "An afterlife definitely exists"; 79 responded, "An afterlife probably exists"; 82 responded, "I was uncertain if an afterlife exists"; 16 responded, "An afterlife probably does not exist"; 18 responded, "An afterlife does not exist"; and 34 did not answer about their belief in an afterlife prior to their experience. After their deep NDE, 270 responded, "An afterlife definitely exists"; 12 responded, "An afterlife probably exists"; 8 responded, "I am uncertain if an afterlife exists"; 1 responded, "An afterlife probably does not exist"; 0 responded, "An afterlife does not exist"; and 6 did not give an answer (Long, 2018).

Chapter 6

Conclusion

The well-protected room or very large house that only some are allowed to enter and testify about after being randomly selected to do so is a thought experiment that is worth investigating and developing further in its own right, especially by epistemologists and those interested in the philosophy of testimony. When everyone who has had an experience of something in a defined and standardized circumstance agrees with each other about the cause and content of this experience for a justified reason, why should those of us who have not had that experience be skeptical of their testimonies, especially as they begin to accumulate in the thousands and beyond and are representative of the population as a whole? And to what degree are the potential fence-sitters or dissenters who come out of the room, and their reasons for uncertainty or dissent, relevant to the epistemic impact derived from this thought experiment?

The fact that so many NDErs report their experience as vastly more real than our ordinary understanding of real should also be investigated and discussed further by philosophers for its own sake, especially by epistemologists, metaphysicians, phenomenologists, and those interested in the simulation argument. What better epistemic justification can there be for trusting in any experience, other than the fact that it is vastly more real in every conceivable way than the experience of this life? And is this not precisely the intrinsic quality of the experience thereof that we would expect a higher reality to possess and rely on in immediately convincing newcomers of its metaphysical supremacy?

Subtle NDEs convince many, deep NDEs convince the vast majority, and profound NDEs convince seemingly everyone who has them of the reality of an afterlife for the best possible empirical reason imaginable. There is a clear pattern being observed where the deeper into the experience a person who is representative of the population as a whole generally goes, the much more obvious it generally becomes to them that the NDE is caused by a higher reality and is not a brain-generated hallucination. And at some point in the deeper half of the experience there seems to be a cut-off point beyond which no one comes back from unconvinced that their NDE was caused by a higher reality. Therefore, if we were to have a profound NDE ourselves, we would in all likelihood come back certain of or at the very least believing in the reality of an afterlife based on our experience. It does not matter whether it is you, me, or the most passionate, devout, and dogmatic of fundamaterialists, because the literature is clear on the fact that seemingly everyone who has this experience, even passionate physicalists who are certain to the bone that death is the end of all things for the individual, come back with a changed perspective. The NDE world, it is reported again and again, is too real on every conceivable level to deny once we have had the proper experience of it ourselves.

So what exactly is it about the feelings, reasons, or understandings of the person skeptical of the existence of an afterlife that makes them think that they would not be persuaded by a profound or sufficiently deep NDE, where every single phenomenological reason that they currently have for thinking that this seemingly physical world is real to begin with is completely, categorically, and vastly outclassed by the experience of the NDE world, and where they also experience many of the other beyond the ultradeep future qualities of the NDE world? What makes them think that they would not take more seriously a level of reality that is completely in harmony with the best possible feelings and ways of being that provide the most enjoyment and purpose out of existence? Indeed, when they encounter a world or reality that have mastered these things to perfection, and a world or reality in which they are not afraid of or uncomfortable with these self-evidently wonderful things in the slightest, what makes them think that they would not react like other NDErs have often done before them, and realize how unevolved, primitive, ignorant, fearful, and immature so many people are here by comparison? And what makes them think that they would not have the same justified epistemic reaction as everyone else reliably and predictably have in the figurative manner of a seemingly unending assembly line of people who are representative of the population as a whole? What do they think separates them from the rest of humanity, including their fellow neurosurgeons, neurologists, psychologists, physicians, natural scientists, engineers, agnostics, materialists, avowed and passionate strong atheists and antitheists, extremely skeptical, rational, realistic, and reasonable people, very well educated people, and highly intelligent people, etc.? Or will they just try to appeal to some kind of ultimate no true Scotsman fallacy, and argue that none of the agnostics, materialists, or atheists, etc., that changed their worldview because of their NDE were true, reasonable, rational, sane, and skeptical agnostics, materialists, or atheists, etc., to begin with? If not, what relevant skeptical feeling, reason, or understanding do they have about why an afterlife does not or can not exist, or about why NDEs are not or can not be indicative of it, that one hundred percent of the population do not share, or have not seriously considered or understood? Admittedly not all people are reasonable people, so not all NDErs are reasonable people. But a significant percentage of the population consists of reasonable people, so a significant percentage of NDErs are reasonable people that can seriously consider, understand, and be reached with empirical evidence and rational arguments to the contrary of their current convictions. So given that the NDE can be remembered with phenomenological crystal clarity for years and decades after having the NDE, as if it just happened, what relevant skeptical feeling, reason, or understanding does the person skeptical of the existence of an afterlife seriously think will impress the percentage of NDErs that are reasonable? What relevant skeptical feeling, reason, or understanding does the person skeptical of the existence of an afterlife seriously think will make the reasonable percentage of NDErs come to the conclusion that the persuasiveness of the experientially self-evident ultrareality of the NDE world should not outweigh that skeptical feeling, reason, or understanding if the person skeptical of the existence of an afterlife were to communicate it effectively to the reasonable NDErs? And does the person skeptical of the existence of an afterlife seriously think that everyday life is clearly not a self-evidently more real world than our dreams at night for the very same or similar skeptical feelings, reasons, or understandings?

Furthermore, some skeptics have sometimes made remarks to the effect that if they were to have an NDE, or if they were to die permanently, and realize that NDErs were correct in that there is a wonderful afterlife that they transition to during the initial stages of the dying process, then it would be a happy surprise for them, and that they would love to be wrong. But how, exactly, would it really be a surprise to them? If we were to go into the room, should we really be surprised that such an experience could come our way? If we were to go into the room, should we really be surprised to see what everyone else has reported to have seen and observed? Should we really be surprised when we would come to the very same conclusion as everyone else has done, that the thing in question and the issue at stake really is there? And should we really be surprised when we come to that conclusion for the very same reason that everyone else has done? And similarly, if we were to have a profound NDE, should we really be surprised that such an experience could happen to us as well, when all the data indicates that it could happen to anyone who has a survived proximity to death or who come back to life from the initial stages of the dying process? And if we were to have a profound NDE or die permanently, and during the initial stages of the dying process transition to the afterlife dimension, should we really be surprised to see, observe, and experience the same things that previous profound NDErs have already reported to have seen, observed, and experienced? Should we really be surprised when we would come to the very same conclusion as everyone else has already done, that there really is an afterlife after all? And should we really be surprised when we come to that conclusion for the very same reason that everyone else has done, that everything about the NDE world is self-evidently and vastly more real than everything about the experience of everyday life? How exactly would any of that be surprising, at least on a theoretical level? How would it be surprising in any way, shape, or form that we should experience the same thing as everyone else, and that we should come to the same conclusion as everyone else, and that we should come to that same conclusion for the very same justified reason that everyone else has already done so for? How can we honestly try to make the claim that there is no possible way that someone could have discerned some kind of pattern in advance that would make this seem like something to be thoroughly expected? How can we honestly try to make the claim that absolutely no one could feasibly have guessed this or seen it coming as a matter of extreme probability? How can we honestly try to make the claim that we were thoroughly rational for thinking that our strong feelings of skepticism, or the reasons that we had for that skepticism, were all totally unique and had not been shared or seriously considered by those prior to us having the NDE experience? In light of all of the data that we have on NDEs and the argument being presented in this book, how would our experience, our reaction to that experience, and the reason for that reaction to that experience in any way, shape, or form be sincerely surprising to us?

Of course, NDErs are often empathetic to the fact that people do not believe them, and they freely admit that they would have had the same reaction before their experience as well if others would have tried to tell them of such a thing. Doubting the existence of an afterlife and believing in the exclusivity of the world we see around us on a daily basis is something that I think it is fair to assume comes quite easily to many of us, as the immersive, realistic, and numerous impressive qualities of the experience of everyday life are very persuasive when it comes to making us think and feel that everyday life and this particular universe are all there is, and that this is not a simulated existence. But the experience of everyday life is no more persuasive when it comes to making us think and feel right now that everyday life and this particular universe are all there is than the experience of everyday life also was to all NDErs before their NDEs. And yet, people who are representative of the population as a whole still come back and firmly, sincerely, convincingly, and justifiably maintain statements of the following nature:

> "I knew that what would happen next would be the end of any kind of consciousness or existence. I knew that to be true. The idea of any kind of life after death never entered my mind because I didn't believe in that kind of thing. I knew for certain that there was no such thing as life after death. Only simpleminded people believed in that sort of thing. I didn't believe in ... heaven or ... any other fairy tales. ... Why was I alive? I had wanted oblivion[.] ... 'Could this be a dream?' I kept thinking. 'This has got to be a dream.' But I knew that it wasn't. I was aware that I felt more alert, more aware, and more alive than I had ever felt in my entire life. All my senses were extremely vivid. ... The bright light of the room illuminated every detail in crystal clarity. ... How bizarre to feel all of my senses heightened and alert, as if I had just been born. ... Everything was vividly clear. All of the details of the room

were extremely sharp and distinct. ... I had never viewed the world with such clarity and exactness. Everything was in such extreme focus that it was overwhelming. My sense of taste and touch and temperature were exploding. ... [T]he light was more intense and more beautiful than anything I had ever seen. ... I knew that while it was indescribably brilliant, it wasn't just light. This was a living being[.] ... This loving, luminous being who embraced me knew me intimately. He knew me better than I knew myself. ... My experience ... showed me that there is a vastly greater reality than what I had previously known."[146]

"I had grown up pretty much in the scientific culture of the 20th century, what's called reductive materialism. And I was a card-toting member of that reductive materialist scientific community. That's kind of the conventional wisdom that's out there in science. ... [A]s this pure white light came towards me, it was coming with this perfect musical melody, absolutely beautiful. ... That ... spinning melody ... came towards me, and it opened up like a rip ... into this brilliant ultrareal valley. And I remember ascending up into this valley, up into this brilliant greenery, lush with life, absolutely fertile. ... And I remember how we would dip down and go through that lush greenery, and there would be flowers and blossoms, buds on trees that would open up even as we flew by, I remember the rich textures, and colors beyond the rainbow, and so beautiful. And in that beautiful valley as we would come up and ascend above all that greenery I could see that there were hundreds of souls dancing, ... [They were] dressed in peasant garb, very simple clothing, yet beautiful colors, and tremendous joy and merriment, there were lots of children playing and dogs jumping and it was just a wonderful festival. ... [I]n the velvety black skies above were pure spiritual beings, orbs of golden light, swooping and swirling in formation leaving sparkling golden trails, emanating these hymns, chants, anthems, powerful like a tsunami, wave crescendo after crescendo after crescendo of the

most beautiful music, waves washing through me[.] ... Now the important thing to understand is that that gateway valley was much more real than this world. Far sharper, crisper, and more real than this. This is very dreamlike by comparison."[147]

"[E]verything went black, which is what I expected because I was agnostic or atheistic at the time. I had no belief in anything after or anything like that. So everything went black and then it was as if I had just closed my eyes and opened them again and this time I was above, looking down at what was happening below. ... I didn't see it as a tunnel, I always look at it as like when the Starship Enterprise went into warp speed and the lights went flying by ... and I was going towards this brilliant white light [a] gazillion miles away. ... [This being] made me feel completely loved and accepted, this whole feeling of unconditional love ... goes all through you, and it's like ... feeling the comfort of being rocked in mommy's arms or something like that, even more than that, it was more than anything that I've experienced on Earth. I was thirty at the time this happened, so married, had three children, ... so I had experienced love but not love like this. This is just, there are no words, ineffable as they say. ... [T]his being and I communicated telepathically and any question I had was answered before I could think of the question, it was like a download of information coming to me. ... [A]ll of a sudden we were in this light and it was ... kind of like a camera lens where it opened up and it was like I saw reality. This is not reality. What I saw there was reality and it was like, 'Whoa! Amazing!' ... [W]e don't die, ... the whole thing that we have to realize is we just step out of our body and then ... our consciousness continues on."[148]

"[B]eing agnostic, I assumed that, you know, we just became nothing, you know that when we die there was nothing, ... and that was it. So when I had this deeper intelligence as a spirit, I was shocked, [because] I placed so much emphasis on my brain, *that when my spirit form lifted out of my body, I was like, 'Oh, I'm so clear, this is truly the true me, this spirit form is me, that body on the table is just a bloody piece of meat that they're operating on that I use ... as something to take me through this life. But the real me is the spirit.' And it was so clear over there, like in those first few seconds my intelligence felt more heightened immediately. I felt like I could see the entire room, I could see what the surgeons were doing, I could observe a lot and understand a lot of information all at one time. And you know we're not limited by eyes that look straight ahead, when we're the spirit form we can just see everything. Then I saw these angels[.] ... They were composed of light, they were highly intelligent, and they communicated with telepathy. ... I wasn't afraid, there wasn't a single moment where I was afraid in this experience[.] ... [A] lot of people live in fear of death when they're in the physical body. I understand that. But once you're there, it's not that scary, ... it's just another reality. ... [I] moved on to this beautiful landscape where the grass was beautiful, so deeply green as if nothing had ever touched it, there was no death, no harm, everything was just vibrant with life. ... [I]t was like ... an atomic bomb of love."*[149]

"[T]his feeling was just this exhilarating euphoria. I felt so happy to be home. ... And I couldn't stop thinking, 'How did I forget who I really was? How in the world?' There was such an incredible trick that I was in this body and I was this person because I was no longer [this person]. ... And all of a sudden I landed in a place, and ... there were beings there. There were these three robed guys, and they were overjoyed to see me, they were kidding around and they were bouncing around, and I had known them forever. ... [W]e take [this life] so seriously and it seems so real, and where we're going, where we come from, is so different. It's so light and it's full of love, every living thing. So anyway I did go back and it's the usual story, everyone thought I was crazy ... and after a few weeks you learn to just zip it and keep it to yourself. ... [F]or all you out there that

are looking for answers … and you might be afraid or you might be confused, just keep going. There's never anything to fear, there's no problems here, there's no death. Have fun, and help others."[150]

"*[I]t's just unlimited love[.] … You know how when you slip down into a nice hot bath or a hot tub and you kind of go, 'Ah, this is amazing!' It would be sort of that feeling would be the best [way that] I can describe it. … This was nothing like [a dream]. This I can remember clear as day, as if it happened just moments ago, … I can go to that space and time, right now or anytime I wish to and remember it fully, experience it fully, now. … [T]here is no death, it really is like stepping out of a movie and walking into the next room, sort of like, our life right now is the movie. So when you go to watch a movie in a movie theater, you're very much into the movie, you're very much into what you're watching, you actually even feel like you're there sometimes, you're experiencing it, and then when it ends the lights come on and you get up and walk out with your friends, you're like, 'Oh, that was really fun, what a great movie!' And then you go on about your life. Life is sort of like that. It really is like stepping from one room to another. Or when you're dreaming and you wake up from a dream you remember sort of, 'Oh, I know I was asleep and I know I was dreaming.' And then you wake up from your sleep and all of a sudden you're aware of life again. It's very much like that[.] … [A]nd then you're back into your oneness, your wholeness, and that place is nothing but love. … [W]hen you cross over or when you die it's not scary. It's love, it's beautiful, and it's easy.*"[151]

"*[A]s I got closer to the light, all of a sudden I popped into a giant sphere. It was about the size of a basketball coliseum. And I was suspended in the middle of this sphere, and all around me at all parts of the sphere … were miniature motion pictures of my lives and what was going on. And I could see, I could touch, I could feel, I could sense every emotion that was taking place in all of* those lifetimes. And when I would concentrate on one I would immediately be there, I would be reliving what I had lived, and I would remember the reliving, and then I would think about another area and then I pop into another movie. ... The light absorbed me into the light, so I was part of the light. And once I was in the light I knew everything the light knew. I knew all about the universe, I knew everything about flowers, about plants, about asteroids, about suns, about novas, everything. I didn't have a question for the light. Why? Because I knew all the answers. I had nothing to ask. And we laughed and we played, and by the way the light has a fantastic sense of humor. We reviewed some of the really silly things that I did in my lifetime and we'd be laughing at how serious I took them. Because life down here is an illusion, it's a game. Don't take it so [seriously]."[152]

"When I came into this place [there were] colors I've never seen before. ... This guy was a blue I've never seen before. It was vibrant, and the white was pure, I mean nothing, there is no way to describe that white. The whitest thing I could ever see anywhere doesn't come close to this white that I saw there, it's just, there's no comparison. And the colors were vibrant, I don't know how else to say it and I have never seen them here. ... [W]hat I saw there was, beautiful is not as strong, I don't know, it was so intensely wonderful, powerful, everything you think it is and more. ... It's so wonderful, pain-free, perfect there. ... All of us are going to pass away and all of us are going to die at some point, so when you do get there, it's different, it's this whole other thing, and you're not going to want to leave, it's wonderful and it's beautiful. ... [C]oming back you see everything different, you see people different. I am so not scared of so many things out there now and like you have no idea how much this is just not a big deal and your perspective is just so different. ... To know that when you die it's not the end, it's just not. This is like one small stepping stone to after, this just is a tiny piece of it. ... I *know this is not a farce, but it's school, it's, I mean, we're all here to learn, we're all here to do better and be better, how you treat others and stuff.*"[153]

"[T]he next thing I knew I was in this other dimension of heaven, and it was real, and it wasn't my brain shutting down. It was a real experience. When I was there, loved ones that I knew only in heaven ... were there to greet me and they were there to welcome and hold me and love and tell me it'll be okay. And I remember feeling this overwhelming love and peace. ... [A]nd I had a life review, I went through my life ... and I could feel what other people felt that I had experienced life with, as well as [what] I experienced ... and [what] bystanders would feel, and I could choose to go to whatever part of my life I wanted to to learn and grow from that experience. ... We judge ourselves, and it's not really a judgment, it's a learning episode, life is a learning episode for us. We are here to learn and grow and to become better and learn empathy and compassion and love for others and learn from our wrongdoings of what we did on Earth, because we've all done them. ... They showed me that we choose our parents and we choose our life and we choose our hardships and we come down multiple times by choice, not by force, to learn and grow from the experiences to make us better spirits."[154]

"There were about two hundred fifty to three hundred people there waiting to see me. Oh my god, they were thrilled to meet me! They all hugged me, they all kissed me. The women, do you remember the Breck girl commercials? ... They were all shiny just like that, okay, and the men too, the men were just radiant. ... Just beauty, shining, energy, love, that was it. ... And clearly this was paradise."[155]

"It is difficult to adapt to Earth after coming back from a much higher and evolved place. ... One life on Earth is just a flash of our

existence, a photo among thousands."[156]

"[E]ven though this world is amazing, NDErs when they experience this amount of peace and love in spirit, they come back and they realize, 'Why are we not like that here? Why are we still not evolved more?' ... I mean really this is basically the Matrix, that's exactly what we're living in."[157]

"And all of a sudden I found myself in a long hallway of doors. There one was this beautiful, Gothic looking wood door, and as I would peer through the door, I would literally see an existence that I was participating in."[158]

Testimonies that are similar to these by people who are representative of the population as a whole go on and on and on (and on), with no end in sight. In these we can clearly discern how the NDE often changed their view on the existence of an afterlife, and also discern the various realer than real attributes of the experience. Furthermore and as alluded to earlier, at least some NDErs were equally as skeptical of the existence of an afterlife or of the idea that NDEs are or can be indicative of an afterlife as we may be now, and at least some of them also shared the intensity of that skepticism, and at least some of them also shared whatever justifications we may think or feel that we have for that skepticism. And yet, the NDE thoroughly and justifiably convinced them that there really is an afterlife for experientially self-evident and realer than real attributes of the experience.

Of course, and as alluded to in the introduction of this book, sometimes our rock solid feelings of skepticism or incredulity can not be overcome merely by arguments or by data, or by both, no matter how objectively persuasive the arguments or the data may be. Furthermore, our experiential unfamiliarity with what having an NDE is actually like, or our inability to imagine what it is like to have an NDE, certainly does not make it easier to accept and believe that an afterlife in all likelihood actually exists. Sometimes, for some of us, our minds will simply not let us actually accept and believe in something, no matter what. But in light of these four well-established facts regarding the NDE and the thought experiment and analysis I have herein provided, do we have any rational or empirical justification for thinking that millions or tens of millions of converging testimonies on the matter by people who are representative of the population as a whole, with the best possible empirical justification imaginable for their assertion, must somehow all be likely lying, mistaken, or irrelevant, or any combination thereof? Or is there, indeed, a shining pink elephant in the room that we are all just too afraid to acknowledge?

Notes

1. See for instance Carter, *Science and the Near-Death Experience: How Consciousness Survives Death*; Parnia et al., "AWARE — AWAreness during REsuscitation — A prospective study"; Rivas et al., *The Self Does Not Die: Verified Paranormal Phenomena from Near-Death Experiences*; van Lommel et al., "Near-death Experience in Survivors of Cardiac Arrest: A Prospective Study in the Netherlands."

2. See for instance Grossman, "Book Review," Review of *The Handbook of Near-Death Experiences: Thirty Years of Investigation*; Grossman, "Book Review," Review of *The Self Does Not Die: Verified Paranormal Phenomena From Near-Death Experiences*; Perry, "Why Do Near-death Experiences Seem So Real?"; Ring, "Response to Augustine's 'Does Paranormal Perception Occur in Near-Death Experiences?'", 75-76.

3. Ring, "Response to Augustine's 'Does Paranormal Perception Occur in Near-Death Experiences?'", 75-76.

4. Perry, "Why Do Near-death Experiences Seem So Real?", 476, 481.

5. Grossman, "Book Review," Review of *The Self Does Not Die: Verified Paranormal Phenomena From Near-Death Experiences*, 248-249.

6. Ring, "Response to Augustine's 'Does Paranormal Perception Occur in Near-Death Experiences?'", 70-71.

7. Grossman, "Who's Afraid of Life After Death?", 9.

8. Grossman, "Four Errors Commonly Made by Professional Debunkers," 227-228.

9. Grossman, "Who's Afraid of Life After Death?", 12-13.

10. Holden, "Transpersonal Experiences: Responding Therapeutically," 147; Holden et al., "Characteristics of Western Near-Death Experiencers," 133; Parnia et

al., "AWARE—AWAreness during REsuscitation—A prospective study"; van Lommel et al., "Near-death Experience in Survivors of Cardiac Arrest: A Prospective Study in the Netherlands."

11. Greyson, "The Near-Death Experience Scale. Construction, Reliability, and Validity"; Khanna and Greyson, "Near-Death Experiences and Spiritual Well-Being"; Parnia, *What Happens When We Die: A Groundbreaking Study into the Nature of Life and Death*, 15-18; Ring, *Life at Death: A Scientific Investigation of the Near-Death Experience*.

12. Flynn, "Meanings and Implications of NDEr Transformations: Some Preliminary Findings and Implications"; Groth-Marnat and Summers, "Altered Beliefs, Attitudes, and Behaviors Following Near-Death Experiences"; Musgrave, "The Near-Death Experience: A Study of Spiritual Transformation"; Schwaninger et al., "A Prospective Analysis of Near-Death Experiences in Cardiac Arrest Patients"; Steadman, *Aspects of near-death experiences that bring about life change*; Sutherland, "Changes in Religious Beliefs, Attitudes, and Practices Following Near-Death Experiences: An Australian Study"; Tassell-Matamua and Murray, "Near-Death Experiences: Quantitative Findings from an Aotearoa New Zealand Sample"; van Lommel, *Consciousness Beyond Life: The Science of the Near-Death Experience*, 54-55; van Lommel et al., "Near-death Experience in Survivors of Cardiac Arrest: A Prospective Study in the Netherlands."

13. Greyson et al., "Explanatory Models for Near-Death Experiences," 228; Long and Perry, *Evidence of the Afterlife: The Science of Near-Death Experiences*, 2, 102; Moore and Greyson, "Characteristics of Memories for Near-Death Experiences"; Palmieri et al., "'Reality' of near-death experience memories: evidence from a psychodynamic and electrophysiological integrated study"; Perry, "Why Do

Near-death Experiences Seem So Real?"; Stout et al., "Six Major Challenges Faced by Near-Death Experiencers"; Thonnard et al., "Characteristics of Near-Death Experiences Memories as Compared to Real and Imagined Events Memories."

14. Gallup and Proctor, *Adventures in Immortality: A Look Beyond the Threshold of Death*; Grey, *Return from Death: An Exploration of the Near-death Experience*; Greyson, "Near-Death Experiences Precipitated by Suicide Attempt: Lack of Influence of Psychopathology, Religion, and Expectations"; Greyson, "Incidence and Correlates of Near-Death Experiences in a Cardiac Care Unit"; Greyson, "Near-Death Experiences and Spirituality"; Grossman, "Book Review," Review of *The Handbook of Near-Death Experiences: Thirty Years of Investigation*; Grossman, "Book Review," Review of *The Self Does Not Die: Verified Paranormal Phenomena From Near-Death Experiences*; Holden, "Transpersonal Experiences: Responding Therapeutically," 147; Holden et al., "Characteristics of Western Near-Death Experiencers," 133; McLaughlin and Malony, "Near-death Experiences and Religion: A Further Investigation"; Osis and Haraldsson, *At the Hour of Death*; Ring, *Life at Death: A Scientific Investigation of the Near-Death Experience*; Sabom, *Recollections of Death: A Medical Investigation*; van Lommel et al., "Near-death Experience in Survivors of Cardiac Arrest: A Prospective Study in the Netherlands."

15. Gallup and Proctor, *Adventures in Immortality: A Look Beyond the Threshold of Death*; Knoblauch et al., "Different Kinds of Near-Death Experience: A Report on a Survey of Near-Death Experiences in Germany"; Pasricha, "Near-Death Experiences in India: Prevalence and New Features"; Perera et al., "Prevalence of Near-Death Experiences in Australia"; Rominger, "Exploring the Integration of Near-Death Experience Aftereffects: Summary of Findings"; van

Lommel, *Consciousness Beyond Life: The Science of the Near-Death Experience*, 108-109.

16. Adler, "Epistemological problems of testimony"; Coady, *Testimony: A Philosophical Study*; Shapin, *A Social History of Truth: Civility and Science in Seventeenth-Century England*.

17. Grossman, "Four Errors Commonly Made by Professional Debunkers."

18. Sutherland, "'Trailing Clouds of Glory': The Near-Death Experiences of Western Children and Teens," 92-93, 105-107.

19. Adler, "Epistemological problems of testimony"; Shapin, *A Social History of Truth: Civility and Science in Seventeenth-Century England*.

20. Talwar and Lee, "Social and Cognitive Correlates of Children's Lying Behavior."

21. Fanelli, "How Many Scientists Fabricate and Falsify Research? A Systematic Review and Meta-Analysis of Survey Data."

22. Sagan, *Broca's Brain: Reflections on the Romance of Science*; Voss et al., "Extraordinary Claims Require Extraordinary Evidence: A Comment on Cozzuol et al. (2013)," 893.

23. Carter, *Science and Psychic Phenomena: The Fall of the House of Skeptics*, 210-224, 239-246; Deming, "Do Extraordinary Claims Require Extraordinary Evidence?"

24. Parnia et al., "AWARE—AWAreness during REsuscitation—A prospective study"; Rivas et al., *The Self Does Not Die: Verified Paranormal Phenomena from Near-Death Experiences*.

25. Grossman, "Who's Afraid of Life After Death?"

26. Carter, *Science and the Near-Death Experience: How Consciousness Survives Death*, 105, 246-247.

27. Charlier, "Oldest Medical Description of a Near Death Experience (NDE), France, 18th Century"; Holden et al., "The Field of Near-Death Studies: Past, Present, and

Future"; Shushan, *Conceptions of the Afterlife in Early Civilizations: Universalism, Constructivism and Near-Death Experience.*

28. Long and Perry, *Evidence of the Afterlife: The Science of Near-Death Experiences*, 135-147; Sutherland, "'Trailing Clouds of Glory': The Near-Death Experiences of Western Children and Teens", 87-107.

29. Carter, *Science and the Near-Death Experience: How Consciousness Survives Death*, 136-149; Long and Perry, *Evidence of the Afterlife: The Science of Near-Death Experiences*, 149-171.

30. "Peter Panagore's NDE and Why He Regretted Coming Back."

31. Moorjani, *Dying To Be Me: My Journey from Cancer, to Near Death, to True Healing*, 109, 111.

32. "Living without fear of Dying, Near Death Experience, Crossing Over, Free will to leave."

33. "Dr. Jeffrey Long - Near Death Experiences."

34. Ring, *Waiting to Die: A Near-Death Researcher's (Mostly Humorous) Reflections on His Own Endgame*, 33.

35. Ring, *Waiting to Die: A Near-Death Researcher's (Mostly Humorous) Reflections on His Own Endgame*, 33.

36. Ring, *Waiting to Die: A Near-Death Researcher's (Mostly Humorous) Reflections on His Own Endgame*, 33.

37. Ring, *Waiting to Die: A Near-Death Researcher's (Mostly Humorous) Reflections on His Own Endgame*, 33.

38. "Dr. Jeffrey Long - Near Death Experiences."

39. "Conversations with NDErs With Nancy Rynes-- Episode #28."

40. Groth-Marnat and Summers, "Altered Beliefs, Attitudes, and Behaviors Following Near-Death Experiences."

41. Ring, *Waiting to Die: A Near-Death Researcher's (Mostly Humorous) Reflections on His Own Endgame*, 99.

42. Ring, *Waiting to Die: A Near-Death Researcher's (Mostly*

Humorous) Reflections on His Own Endgame, 99.

43. Ring, *Waiting to Die: A Near-Death Researcher's (Mostly Humorous) Reflections on His Own Endgame*, 99.

44. Ring, *Waiting to Die: A Near-Death Researcher's (Mostly Humorous) Reflections on His Own Endgame*, 99.

45. Ring, *Waiting to Die: A Near-Death Researcher's (Mostly Humorous) Reflections on His Own Endgame*, 99.

46. Ring, *Waiting to Die: A Near-Death Researcher's (Mostly Humorous) Reflections on His Own Endgame*, 99.

47. Ring, *Waiting to Die: A Near-Death Researcher's (Mostly Humorous) Reflections on His Own Endgame*, 99.

48. "Present! - Raymond Kinman's Near-Death Experience."

49. "Beyond Death - Brooklyn College - near death experiences documentary."

50. Kean, *Surviving Death: A Journalist Investigates Evidence for an Afterlife*, 107.

51. Sutherland, "Changes in Religious Beliefs, Attitudes, and Practices Following Near-Death Experiences: An Australian Study," 29.

52. Carter, *Science and the Near-Death Experience: How Consciousness Survives Death*, 6-102.

53. Grossman, "Who's Afraid of Life After Death?"

54. Carter, *Science and the Near-Death Experience: How Consciousness Survives Death*, 6-102.

55. Soothill, *The Three Religions of China: Lectures Delivered at Oxford*, 75.

56. Bostrom, "Are We Living in a Computer Simulation?"

57. "Nanci Danison Interview - Part 3."

58. "What is the meaning of life? - Near Death Experience - of Wayne Morrison."

59. "NDE Steve."

60. N., Jesse, "Jesse N NDE 2809."

61. "The Day I Died! My Near Death Experience!"

62. "Near Death Experience - Evidence Against Naturalism

(Part 7)."

63. "Past Lives Podcast Ep45 Jan Holden."

64. Moore and Greyson, "Characteristics of Memories for Near-Death Experiences," 121-122.

65. Grossman, "Who's Afraid of Life After Death?"

66. Hoffman, "Disclosure Needs and Motives After a Near-Death Experience"; Hoffman, "Disclosure Habits After Near-Death Experiences: Influences, Obstacles, and Listener Selection"; Sartori, *The Wisdom of Near-Death Experiences: How Understanding NDEs Can Help Us Live More Fully*, 152-153.

67. Parnia et al., "AWARE—AWAreness during REsuscitation—A prospective study"; Rivas et al., *The Self Does Not Die: Verified Paranormal Phenomena from Near-Death Experiences*.

68. Grossman, "Book Review," Review of *The Handbook of Near-Death Experiences: Thirty Years of Investigation*.

69. Blackmore, *Dying to Live: Near-Death Experiences*, 136-164.

70. Fischer and Mitchell-Yellin, *Near-Death Experiences: Understanding Visions of the Afterlife*, 33-45.

71. Fosse et al., "Dreaming and Episodic Memory: A Functional Dissociation?"; Hobson et al., "The Neuropsychology of REM Sleep Dreaming."

72. "Episode 121 'The Athiest [sic] Who Went to Heaven' Nancy Rynes on We Don't Die Radio Show."

73. Storm, *Howard Storm's Near-Death Experience*.

74. Andréason, *Spirituality*.

75. "Near Death Experience - Death before Graduation, Back Again."

76. "Present! - Raymond Kinman's Near-Death Experience."

77. "Life After Death Experience (NDE) with Steve Gardipee, Vietnam War Story | One of the Best NDEs."

78. "12/23/2019 - Angela Williams."

79. "Peter Panagore's NDE and Why He Regretted Coming

Back."

80. N., Jesse, "Jesse N NDE 2809."

81. F., Mary Ann, "Mary Ann F NDE 563."

82. The divine Love we share between us is all that truly matters and is measured and endures, *The divine Love we share between us is all that truly matters and is measured and endures.*

83. W., Martin, "Martin W NDE 8303."

84. "Ian McCormick - After death Experience."

85. L., Laurie, "Laurie L NDE 8525."

86. "HEAVEN IS REAL BECAUSE I'VE BEEN THERE.."

87. Perry, "Why Do Near-death Experiences Seem So Real?", 478.

88. "Episode 197 Daniel Berdichevsky - Shares his NDE and 'Questions & Answers from God' on We Don't Die."

89. "How Unconditional Love Feels."

90. F., Rachel, "Rachel F NDE 8805."

91. "Present! - Raymond Kinman's Near-Death Experience."

92. Andréason, *Spirituality*.

93. "Girl has near death experience – amazing."

94. ""Life After Death" with Diane Sawyer - ABC News Turning Point."

95. "Kenneth Ring - Near Death Experiences, Part 1."

96. Perry, "Why Do Near-death Experiences Seem So Real?", 478.

97. Perry, "Why Do Near-death Experiences Seem So Real?", 479.

98. Alexander, *Proof of Heaven: A Neurosurgeon's Journey into the Afterlife*, 45-46.

99. "Prophetic Voices Documentary: Kenneth Ring Interviews Four Near-Death Experiencers."

100. "Present! - Raymond Kinman's Near-Death Experience."

101. "Amphianda's NDE."

102. "Dr. Mary Neal's Near Death Experience & Joyful Lessons

for Everyone."

103. Storm, *Howard Storm's Near-Death Experience.*

104. "Ian McCormick - After death Experience."

105. The divine Love we share between us is all that truly matters and is measured and endures, *The divine Love we share between us is all that truly matters and is measured and endures.*

106. Perry, "Why Do Near-death Experiences Seem So Real?", 477-478.

107. Stevenson and Cook, "Involuntary Memories During Severe Physical Illness or Injury"; Zingrone and Alvarado, "Pleasurable Western Adult Near-Death Experiences: Features, Circumstances, and Incidence," 22.

108. Long and Perry, *Evidence of the Afterlife: The Science of Near-Death Experiences*, 107-116.

109. *The Day I Died: The Mind, the Brain, and Near-Death Experiences.*

110. The divine Love we share between us is all that truly matters and is measured and endures, *The divine Love we share between us is all that truly matters and is measured and endures.*

111. "The Life Review."

112. Andréason, *Spirituality.*

113. "Dr. Jeffrey Long - Near Death Experiences."

114. "Answers From The Afterlife with Nanci L. Danison."

115. "Episode 197 Daniel Berdichevsky - Shares his NDE and 'Questions & Answers from God' on We Don't Die."

116. "Life is like a Haunted House."

117. "Near Death Experience - In The Realm of God."

118. *The Day I Died: The Mind, the Brain, and Near-Death Experiences.*

119. "Prophetic Voices Documentary: Kenneth Ring Interviews Four Near-Death Experiencers."

120. "Amphianda's NDE."

121. *The Day I Died: The Mind, the Brain, and Near-Death Experiences.*

122. "Near Death Experience: Brilliant white Light - Part 1."

123. "Rich Kelley near death experience."

124. Andréason, *Spirituality.*

125. Stout et al., "Six Major Challenges Faced by Near-Death Experiencers," 52.

126. Parnia et al., "AWARE—AWAreness during REsuscitation—A prospective study"; Rivas et al., *The Self Does Not Die: Verified Paranormal Phenomena from Near-Death Experiences.*

127. Moore and Greyson, "Characteristics of Memories for Near-Death Experiences"; Palmieri et al., "'Reality' of near-death experience memories: evidence from a psychodynamic and electrophysiological integrated study"; Thonnard et al., "Characteristics of Near-Death Experiences Memories as Compared to Real and Imagined Events Memories."

128. Greyson, "Consistency of Near-Death Experience Accounts Over Two Decades: Are Reports Embellished Over Time?"

129. Grossman, "Four Errors Commonly Made by Professional Debunkers."

130. Alexander, *Proof of Heaven: A Neurosurgeon's Journey into the Afterlife*, 39, 130.

131. Holden et al., "Characteristics of Western Near-Death Experiencers," 133.

132. Wright, *Knowledge Transmission.*

133. Ring, *Life at Death: A Scientific Investigation of the Near-Death Experience.*

134. Greyson, "The Near-Death Experience Scale. Construction, Reliability, and Validity."

135. Parnia, *What Happens When We Die: A Groundbreaking Study into the Nature of Life and Death*, 17.

136. Khanna and Greyson, "Near-Death Experiences and Spiritual Well-Being"; Steadman, *Aspects of near-death*

experiences that bring about life change.

137. Groth-Marnat and Summers, "Altered Beliefs, Attitudes, and Behaviors Following Near-Death Experiences"; Schwaninger et al., "A Prospective Analysis of Near-Death Experiences in Cardiac Arrest Patients"; Steadman, *Aspects of near-death experiences that bring about life change*; Sutherland, "Changes in Religious Beliefs, Attitudes, and Practices Following Near-Death Experiences: An Australian Study"; Tassell-Matamua and Murray, "Near-Death Experiences: Quantitative Findings from an Aotearoa New Zealand Sample."

138. Bush, "Distressing Western Near-Death Experiences: Finding a Way through the Abyss"; Carter, *Science and the Near-Death Experience: How Consciousness Survives Death*, 127-135.

139. Parnia et al., "AWARE—AWAreness during REsuscitation—A prospective study"; van Lommel et al., "Near-death Experience in Survivors of Cardiac Arrest: A Prospective Study in the Netherlands."

140. Bush and Greyson, "Distressing Near-Death Experiences: The Basics"; Grey, *Return from Death: An Exploration of the Near-death Experience*, 72.

141. Groth-Marnat and Summers, "Altered Beliefs, Attitudes, and Behaviors Following Near-Death Experiences"; Steadman, *Aspects of near-death experiences that bring about life change*; van Lommel et al., "Near-death Experience in Survivors of Cardiac Arrest: A Prospective Study in the Netherlands."

142. Greyson, "Incidence and Correlates of Near-Death Experiences in a Cardiac Care Unit"; Schwaninger et al., "A Prospective Analysis of Near-Death Experiences in Cardiac Arrest Patients."

143. Greyson, "Near-Death Experiences Precipitated by Suicide Attempt: Lack of Influence of Psychopathology, Religion,

and Expectations"; van Lommel et al., "Near-death Experience in Survivors of Cardiac Arrest: A Prospective Study in the Netherlands."

144. Steadman, *Aspects of near-death experiences that bring about life change.*

145. Moore and Greyson, "Characteristics of Memories for Near-Death Experiences."

146. Storm, *My Descent Into Death: A Second Chance at Life*, 9-10, 12, 25, 72.

147. "Eben Alexander: A Neurosurgeon's Journey through the Afterlife."

148. "Diane Goble Pt 1 Near Death Experiences."

149. "Tricia Barker Shaman Oaks."

150. "Present! - Bill Letson's Near-Death Experience (and Ayahuasca)."

151. "Near Death Experience Brief Description."

152. "Near Death Experience - Death before Graduation, Back Again."

153. "Susan Noeske NDE - Suicide is Cheating."

154. "NDE to bring Love and Hope."

155. "Near Death Experience: 'This was Paradise'."

156. B., Sarah, "Sarah B NDEs 8935."

157. "LIFE AFTER A NEAR-DEATH EXPERIENCE (possible outcomes)."

158. *Heaven's Tourist*, 2005.

References

"12/23/2019 - Angela Williams" (2020) YouTube video, added by NDE Radio with Lee Witting [Online]. Available at www.youtube.com/watch?v=0E5pdB69kao (Accessed 15 September 2020).

Adler, J. (2017) "Epistemological problems of testimony." *The Stanford Encyclopedia of Philosophy* (Winter 2017 Edition), Zalta, E. N. (ed) [Online]. Available at plato.stanford.edu/archives/win2017/entries/testimony-episprob/ (Accessed 4 May 2018).

"Agnostic Dies and Meets God - Tricia Barker's NDE" (2020) YouTube video, added by Shaman Oaks [Online]. Available at www.youtube.com/watch?v=UEnE61R_aLI (Accessed 19 September 2020).

Alexander, E. (2012) *Proof of Heaven: A Neurosurgeon's Journey into the Afterlife*. New York: Simon and Schuster.

"Amphianda's NDE" (2018) YouTube video, added by Amphianda Baskett [Online]. Available at www.youtube.com/watch?v=F7ToAH3Ni40 (Accessed 16 May 2020).

Andréason, C. (2013) *Spirituality* [Online]. Available at allaboutchristian.com/spirituality/index.html (Accessed 2 May 2018).

"Answers From The Afterlife with Nanci L. Danison" (2020) YouTube video, added by OMTimes Media [Online]. Available at www.youtube.com/watch?v=4LA3-mi5mqo (Accessed 16 December 2020).

B., Sarah (2019) "Sarah B NDEs 8935", *Near-Death Experience Research Foundation*, 22 December [Online]. Available at www.nderf.org/Experiences/1sarah_b_ndes.html (Accessed 4 January 2020).

"Beyond Death - Brooklyn College - near death experiences documentary" (2013) YouTube video, added by Brain

Boyle [Online]. Available at www.youtube.com/watch?v=bdb2NuhKAWk (Accessed 9 September 2016).

Blackmore, S. (1993) *Dying to Live: Near-Death Experiences*. Buffalo: Prometheus Books.

Bostrom, N. (2003) "Are We Living in a Computer Simulation?" *Philosophical Quarterly*, vol. 53, no. 211, pp. 243-255.

Bush, N. E. (2009) "Distressing Western Near-Death Experiences: Finding a Way through the Abyss," in Holden, J. M., Greyson, B. and James, D. (eds) *The Handbook of Near-Death Experiences: Thirty Years of Investigation*. Santa Barbara: Praeger/ABC-CLIO, pp. 63-86.

Bush, N. E. and Greyson, B. (2014) "Distressing Near-Death Experiences: The Basics." *Missouri Medicine*, vol. 111, no. 6, pp. 486-490.

Carter, C. (2010) *Science and the Near-Death Experience: How Consciousness Survives Death*. Rochester: Inner Traditions.

Carter, C. (2012) *Science and Psychic Phenomena: The Fall of the House of Skeptics*, 2nd edn. Rochester: Inner Traditions.

Charlier, P. (2009) "Oldest Medical Description of a Near Death Experience (NDE), France, 18th Century" [Letter to the Editor]. *Resuscitation*, vol. 85, no. 9, e155 [Online]. DOI: 10.1016/j.resuscitation.2014.05.039 (Accessed 20 August 2019).

Coady, C. A. J. (1992) *Testimony: A Philosophical Study*. New York: Oxford University Press.

"Conversations with NDErs With Nancy Rynes--Episode #28" (2018) YouTube video, added by Near Death Experience: Healed by the Light [Online]. Available at www.youtube.com/watch?v=VA8IEoAVOAc (Accessed 19 August 2019).

Deming, D. (2016) "Do Extraordinary Claims Require Extraordinary Evidence?" *Philosophia*, vol. 44, no. 4, pp. 1319-1331 [Online]. DOI: 10.1007/s11406-016-9779-7 (Accessed 19 August 2019).

"Diane Goble Pt 1 Near Death Experiences" (2015) YouTube

video, added by Pauline Interviews [Online]. Available at www.youtube.com/watch?v=CWaghAcBLI0 (Accessed 23 May 2016).

"Dr. Jeffrey Long - Near Death Experiences" (2012) YouTube video, added by seektruthandwisdom [Online]. Available at www.youtube.com/watch?v=LwyVFW9kT8k (Accessed 18 June 2013).

"Dr. Mary Neal's Near Death Experience & Joyful Lessons for Everyone" (2020) YouTube video, added by IANDSvideos [Online]. Available at www.youtube.com/watch?v=W2QEXUIYL-U (Accessed 23 December 2020).

"Eben Alexander: A Neurosurgeon's Journey through the Afterlife" (2014) YouTube video, added by Theosophical Society [Online]. Available at www.youtube.com/watch?v=qbkgj5J91hE (Accessed 2 June 2017).

"Episode 121 'The Athiest [sic] Who Went to Heaven' Nancy Rynes on We Don't Die Radio Show" (2016) YouTube video, added by We Don't Die Radio [Online]. Available at www.youtube.com/watch?v=JVre-kl5ePQ (Accessed 17 December 2016).

"Episode 197 Daniel Berdichevsky - Shares his NDE and 'Questions & Answers from God' on We Don't Die" (2017) YouTube video, added by We Don't Die Radio [Online]. Available at www.youtube.com/watch?v=Y3r_IfDDwJI (Accessed 29 May 2018).

F., Mary Ann (2002) "Mary Ann F NDE 563", *Near-Death Experience Research Foundation*, 15 June [Online]. Available at www.nderf.org/Experiences/1mary_anne_f_nde.html (Accessed 15 October 2019).

F., Rachel (2019) "Rachel F NDE 8805", *Near-Death Experience Research Foundation*, 22 May [Online]. Available at www.nderf.org/Experiences/1rachel_f_nde.html (Accessed 7 January 2020).

Fanelli, D. (2009) "How Many Scientists Fabricate and Falsify

Research? A Systematic Review and Meta-Analysis of Survey Data." *PLoS ONE,* vol. 4, no. 5, e5738 [Online]. DOI: 10.1371/journal.pone.0005738 (Accessed 17 August 2019).

Fischer, J. M. and Mitchell-Yellin, B. (2016) *Near-Death Experiences: Understanding Visions of the Afterlife.* New York: Oxford University Press.

Flynn, C. P. (1982) "Meanings and Implications of NDEr Transformations: Some Preliminary Findings and Implications." *Anabiosis: The Journal for Near-Death Studies,* vol. 2, no. 1, pp. 3-14.

Fosse, M. J., Fosse, R., Hobson, J. A. and Stickgold, R. J. (2003) "Dreaming and Episodic Memory: A Functional Dissociation?" *Journal of Cognitive Neuroscience,* vol. 15, no. 1, pp. 1-9 [Online]. DOI: 10.1162/089892903321107774 (Accessed 16 August 2019).

Gallup, G. and Proctor, W. (1982) *Adventures in Immortality: A Look Beyond the Threshold of Death.* New York: McGraw-Hill.

"Girl has near death experience – amazing" (2015) YouTube video, added by Rockguitarnow [Online]. Available at www.youtube.com/watch?v=V-GHrsSqcNw (Accessed 29 May 2019).

Grey, M. (1985) *Return from Death: An Exploration of the Near-death Experience.* Boston: Arkana.

Greyson, B. (1983) "The Near-Death Experience Scale. Construction, Reliability, and Validity." *Journal of Nervous & Mental Disease,* vol. 171, no. 6, pp. 369-375.

Greyson, B. (1991) "Near-Death Experiences Precipitated by Suicide Attempt: Lack of Influence of Psychopathology, Religion, and Expectations." *Journal of Near-Death Studies,* vol. 9, no. 3, pp. 183-188.

Greyson, B. (2003) "Incidence and Correlates of Near-Death Experiences in a Cardiac Care Unit." *General Hospital Psychiatry,* vol. 25, no. 4, pp. 269-276.

Greyson, B. (2006) "Near-Death Experiences and Spirituality."

Zygon, vol. 41, no. 2, pp. 393-414.

Greyson, B. (2007) "Consistency of Near-Death Experience Accounts Over Two Decades: Are Reports Embellished Over Time?" *Resuscitation*, vol. 73, no. 3, pp. 407-411.

Greyson, B., Kelly, E. W. and Kelly, E. F. (2009) "Explanatory Models for Near-Death Experiences," in Holden, J. M., Greyson, B. and James, D. (eds) *The Handbook of Near-Death Experiences: Thirty Years of Investigation*. Santa Barbara: Praeger/ABC-CLIO, pp. 213-234.

Grossman, N. (2002) "Who's Afraid of Life After Death?" [Guest Editorial]. *Journal of Near-Death Studies*, vol. 21, no. 1, pp. 5-24.

Grossman, N. (2008) "Four Errors Commonly Made by Professional Debunkers" [Letter to the Editor]. *Journal of Near-Death Studies*, vol. 26, no. 3, pp. 227-235.

Grossman, N. (2010) "Book Review," Review of *The Handbook of Near-Death Experiences: Thirty Years of Investigation*, by Janice Miner Holden, Bruce Greyson and Debbie James (eds). *Journal of Near-Death Studies*, vol. 28, no. 4. pp. 211-232.

Grossman, N. (2016) "Book Review," Review of *The Self Does Not Die: Verified Paranormal Phenomena from Near-Death Experiences*, by Titus Rivas, Anny Dirven and Rudolf H. Smit. *Journal of Near-Death Studies*, vol. 34, no. 4, pp. 233-250.

Groth-Marnat, G. and Summers, R. (1998) "Altered Beliefs, Attitudes, and Behaviors Following Near-Death Experiences." *Journal of Humanistic Psychology*, vol. 38, no. 3, pp. 110-125.

"HEAVEN IS REAL BECAUSE I'VE BEEN THERE.." (2015) YouTube video, added by Last Frontier Medium [Online]. Available at www.youtube.com/watch?v=rTJt2t9kIMs (Accessed 25 May 2019).

Heaven's Tourist (2005) KPRC-TV/Local 2, 23 May. Available at "Christian Andreason's Near-Death Experience on NBC" (2007) YouTube video, added by AngelBear1111 [Online]. Available at www.youtube.com/watch?v=bw3oaNUR1iI

(Accessed 21 May 2010).

Hobson, J. A., Stickgold, R. and Pace-Schott, E. F. (1998) "The Neuropsychology of REM Sleep Dreaming." *NeuroReport*, vol. 9, no. 3, pp. R1-14.

Hoffman, R. M. (1995) "Disclosure Habits After Near-Death Experiences: Influences, Obstacles, and Listener Selection." *Journal of Near-Death Studies*, vol. 14, no. 1, pp. 29-48.

Hoffman, R. M. (1995) "Disclosure Needs and Motives After a Near-Death Experience." *Journal of Near-Death Studies*, vol. 13, no. 4, pp. 237-266.

Holden, J. M. (2016) "Transpersonal Experiences: Responding Therapeutically," in Foster, R. D. and Holden, J. M. (eds) *Connecting Soul, Spirit, Mind, and Body: A Collection of Spiritual and Religious Perspectives and Practices in Counseling*. Denton: University of North Texas Libraries, pp. 145-154.

Holden, J. M., Greyson, B. and James, D. (2009) "The Field of Near-Death Studies: Past, Present, and Future," in Holden, J. M., Greyson, B. and James, D. (eds) *The Handbook of Near-Death Experiences: Thirty Years of Investigation*. Santa Barbara: Praeger/ABC-CLIO, pp. 1-16.

Holden, J. M., Long, J. and MacLurg, B. J. (2009) "Characteristics of Western Near-Death Experiencers," in Holden, J. M., Greyson, B. and James, D. (eds) *The Handbook of Near-Death Experiences: Thirty Years of Investigation*. Santa Barbara: Praeger/ABC-CLIO, pp. 109-133.

"How Unconditional Love Feels" (2010) YouTube video, added by Nanci Danison [Online]. Available at www.youtube.com/watch?v=J_MNZaCpAws (Accessed 16 February 2020).

"Ian McCormick - After death Experience" (2008) YouTube video, added by Christopher Long [Online]. Available at www.youtube.com/watch?v=19QeKtVxrI4 (Accessed 1 October 2010).

Kean, L. (2017) *Surviving Death: A Journalist Investigates Evidence for an Afterlife*. New York: Crown Archetype.

"Kenneth Ring - Near Death Experiences, Part 1" (2013) YouTube video, added by Douglas Jamieson [Online]. Available at www.youtube.com/watch?v=vu6-h28dkys (Accessed 14 January 2014).

Khanna, S. and Greyson, B. (2013) "Near-Death Experiences and Spiritual Well-Being." *Journal of Religion and Health*, vol. 53, no. 6, pp. 1605-1615.

Knoblauch, H., Schmied, I. and Schnettler, B. (2001) "Different Kinds of Near-Death Experience: A Report on a Survey of Near-Death Experiences in Germany." *Journal of Near-Death Studies*, vol. 20, no. 1, pp. 15-29.

L., Laurie (2018) "Laurie L NDE 8525", *Near-Death Experience Research Foundation*, 15 March [Online]. Available at www.nderf.org/Experiences/1laurie_l_nde.html (Accessed 15 February 2020).

"LIFE AFTER A NEAR-DEATH EXPERIENCE (possible outcomes)" (2017) YouTube video, added by Last Frontier Medium [Online]. Available at www.youtube.com/watch?v=dAawiAi7Gqg (Accessed 7 April 2017).

"Life After Death Experience (NDE) with Steve Gardipee, Vietnam War Story | One of the Best NDEs" (2014) YouTube video, added by Dustin Warncke [Online]. Available at www.youtube.com/watch?v=peMIHK87e6w (Accessed 23 December 2019).

""Life After Death" with Diane Sawyer - ABC News Turning Point" (2013) Vimeo video, added by Joseph Angier [Online]. Available at vimeo.com/79075921 (Accessed 28 August 2015).

"Life is like a Haunted House" (2018) YouTube video, added by Nicole Swann [Online]. Available at www.youtube.com/watch?v=yjGDIqZ0CWA (Accessed 1 November 2018).

"Living without fear of Dying, Near Death Experience, Crossing Over, Free will to leave" (2019) YouTube video, added by Nicole Swann [Online]. Available at www.youtube.com/watch?v=tTUrxDdWUWQ (Accessed 3 April 2019).

Long, J. (2018) Email to Jeffrey Long, 10 June.

Long, J. and Perry, P. (2010) *Evidence of the Afterlife: The Science of Near-Death Experiences*. New York: HarperOne.

McLaughlin, S. A. and Newton Malony, H. (1984) "Near-death Experiences and Religion: A Further Investigation." *Journal of Religion and Health*, vol. 23, no. 2, pp. 149-159.

Moore, L. E. and Greyson, B. (2017) "Characteristics of Memories for Near-Death Experiences." *Consciousness and Cognition*, vol. 51, pp. 116-124.

Moorjani, A. (2012) *Dying To Be Me: My Journey from Cancer, to Near Death, to True Healing*. London: Hay House.

Musgrave, C. (1997) "The Near-Death Experience: A Study of Spiritual Transformation." *Journal of Near-Death Studies*, vol. 15, no. 3, pp. 187-201.

N., Jesse (2006) "Jesse N NDE 2809", *Near-Death Experience Research Foundation*, 10 November [Online]. Available at www.nderf.org/Experiences/1jesse_n_nde.html (Accessed 13 October 2010).

"Nanci Danison Interview - Part 3" (2009) YouTube video, added by Nanci Danison [Online]. Available at www.youtube.com/watch?v=BgEOvZldRC8 (Accessed 3 June 2013).

"NDE Steve" (2011) YouTube video, added by Brian Garrett [Online]. Available at www.youtube.com/watch?v=pOGxD_2F5dg (Accessed 22 June 2011).

"NDE to bring Love and Hope" (2020) YouTube video, added by Ashley M. [Online]. Available at www.youtube.com/watch?v=h2CrQdqGqEs (Accessed 27 July 2020).

"Near Death Experience Brief Description" (2017) YouTube video, added by Nicole Swann [Online]. Available at www.youtube.com/watch?v=Bo9IAGeYG7A (Accessed 30 August 2017).

"Near Death Experience: Brilliant white Light - Part 1" (2009) YouTube video, added by LightBehindGod [Online]. Available at www.youtube.com/watch?v=j2y5soNE8KU

(Accessed 27 November 2019).

"Near Death Experience - Death before Graduation, Back Again" (2008) YouTube video, added by billsvideos123 [Online]. Available at www.youtube.com/watch?v=7s0SivLkYTA (Accessed 29 May 2013).

"Near Death Experience - Evidence Against Naturalism (Part 7)" (2008) YouTube video, added by Prophetes [Online]. Available at www.youtube.com/watch?v=ppHlhPr4KbE (Accessed 13 June 2013).

"Near Death Experience - In The Realm of God" (2008) YouTube video, added by billsvideos123 [Online]. Available at www.youtube.com/watch?v=Nzz-nG5pjFg (Accessed 17 July 2008).

"Near Death Experience: 'This was Paradise'" (2009) YouTube video, added by LightBehindGod [Online]. Available at www.youtube.com/watch?v=8UlsbfU7U_8 (Accessed 22 June 2011).

Osis, K. and Haraldsson, E. (1977) *At the Hour of Death*. New York: Avon.

Palmieri, A., Calvo, V., Kleinbub, J. R., Meconi, F., Marangoni, M., Barilaro, P., Broggio, A., Sambin, M. and Sessa, P. (2014) "'Reality' of near-death experience memories: evidence from a psychodynamic and electrophysiological integrated study." *Frontiers in Human Neuroscience*, vol. 8, art. 429 [Online]. DOI: 10.3389/fnhum.2014.00429 (Accessed 1 May 2018).

Parnia, S. (2008) *What Happens When We Die: A Groundbreaking Study into the Nature of Life and Death*, 2nd edn. London: Hay House.

Parnia, S., Spearpoint, K., de Vos, G., Fenwick, P., Goldberg, D., Yang, J., Zhu, J., Baker, K., Killingback, H., McLean, P., Wood, M., Zafari, A. M., Dickert, N., Beisteiner, R., Sterz, F., Berger, M., Warlow, C., Bullock, S., Lovett, S., Metcalfe Smith McPara, R., Marti-Navarette, S., Cushing, P., Wills, P., Harris, K., Sutton, J., Walmsley, A., Deakin, C. D., Little, P., Farber, M., Greyson, B. and Schoenfeld, E. R. (2014)

"AWARE—AWAreness during REsuscitation—A prospective study." *Resuscitation*, vol. 85, no. 12, pp. 1799-1805 [Online]. DOI: 10.1016/j.resuscitation.2014.09.004 (Accessed 2 May 2018).

Pasricha, S. K. (2008) "Near-Death Experiences in India: Prevalence and New Features." *Journal of Near-Death Studies*, vol. 26, no. 4, pp. 267-282.

"Past Lives Podcast Ep45 Jan Holden" (2019) YouTube video, added by The Past Lives Podcast [Online]. Available at www.youtube.com/watch?v=IUaDtvckIME (Accessed 23 September 2020).

Perera, M., Padmasekara, G. and Belanti, J. (2005) "Prevalence of Near-Death Experiences in Australia." *Journal of Near-Death Studies*, vol. 24, no. 2, pp. 109-116.

Perry, R. (2011) "Why Do Near-death Experiences Seem So Real?" [Letter to the Editor]. *Journal of Near-Death Studies*, vol. 29, no. 4, pp. 476–481.

"Peter Panagore's NDE and Why He Regretted Coming Back" (2020) YouTube video, added by Shaman Oaks [Online]. Available at www.youtube.com/watch?v=R8o2rcWldWk (Accessed 7 May 2020).

"Present!-Bill Letson's Near-Death Experience (and Ayahuasca)" (2019) YouTube video, added by Mel Van Dusen [Online]. Available at www.youtube.com/watch?v=roFYMJnSTZA (Accessed 29 November 2019).

"Present! - Raymond Kinman's Near-Death Experience" (2014) YouTube video, added by KMVT [Online]. Available at www.youtube.com/watch?v=tgYHxrBn5Ao (Accessed 4 June 2018).

"Prophetic Voices Documentary: Kenneth Ring Interviews Four Near-Death Experiencers" (2019) YouTube video, added by NewHeaven NewEarth [Online]. Available at www.youtube.com/watch?v=9kWFGgCCYVw (Accessed 27 October 2019).

"Rich Kelley near death experience" (2014) YouTube video, added by Karen Kelley [Online]. Available at www.youtube.

com/watch?v=v2NLEYHjG1g (Accessed 20 May 2015).

Ring, K. (1980) *Life at Death: A Scientific Investigation of the Near-Death Experience*. New York: Coward, McCann and Geoghegan.

Ring, K. (2007) "Response to Augustine's 'Does Paranormal Perception Occur in Near-Death Experiences?'" [Letter to the Editor]. *Journal of Near-Death Studies*, vol. 26, no. 1, pp. 70-76.

Ring, K. (2019) *Waiting to Die: A Near-Death Researcher's (Mostly Humorous) Reflections on His Own Endgame*. Tucson: Wheatmark.

Rivas, T., Dirven, A. and Smit, R. H. (2016) *The Self Does Not Die: Verified Paranormal Phenomena from Near-Death Experiences*. Durham: International Association for Near-Death Studies.

Rominger, R. A. (2009) "Exploring the Integration of Near-Death Experience Aftereffects: Summary of Findings." *Journal of Near-Death Studies*, vol. 28, no. 1, pp. 3-34.

Sabom, M. B. (1982) *Recollections of Death: A Medical Investigation*. New York: Harper and Row.

Sagan, C. (1979) *Broca's Brain: Reflections on the Romance of Science*. New York: Random House.

Sartori, P. (2014) *The Wisdom of Near-Death Experiences: How Understanding NDEs Can Help Us Live More Fully*. Oxford: Watkins Publishing.

Schwaninger, J., Eisenberg, P. R., Schechtman, K. B. and Weiss, A. N. (2002) "A Prospective Analysis of Near-Death Experiences in Cardiac Arrest Patients." *Journal of Near-Death Studies*, vol. 20, no. 4, pp. 215-232.

Shapin, S. (1994) *A Social History of Truth: Civility and Science in Seventeenth-Century England*. Chicago: University of Chicago Press.

Shushan, G. (2009) *Conceptions of the Afterlife in Early Civilizations: Universalism, Constructivism and Near-Death Experience*. London: Continuum.

Soothill, W. E. (1913) *The Three Religions of China: Lectures*

Delivered at Oxford. London: Hodder and Stoughton.

Steadman, K. (2015) *Aspects of near-death experiences that bring about life change*. Master thesis, Palmerston North, Massey University.

Stevenson, I. and Cook, E. W. (1995) "Involuntary Memories During Severe Physical Illness or Injury." *Journal of Nervous and Mental Disease*, vol. 183, no. 7, pp. 452-458.

Storm, H. (2005) *My Descent Into Death: A Second Chance at Life*. New York: Doubleday.

Storm, H. (2016) *Howard Storm's Near-Death Experience* [Online]. Available at www.near-death.com/religion/christianity/ howard-storm.html (Accessed 12 November 2020).

Stout, Y. M., Jacquin, L. A. and Atwater, P. M. H. (2006) "Six Major Challenges Faced by Near-Death Experiencers." *Journal of Near-Death Studies*, vol. 25, no. 1, pp. 49-62.

"Susan Noeske NDE - Suicide is Cheating" (2016) YouTube video, added by Believe it or not #4 [Online]. Available at www.youtube.com/watch?v=Oo7ujk77ASc (Accessed 12 February 2018).

Sutherland, C. (1990) "Changes in Religious Beliefs, Attitudes, and Practices Following Near-Death Experiences: An Australian Study." *Journal of Near-Death Studies*, vol. 9, no. 1, pp. 21-31.

Sutherland, C. (2009) "'Trailing Clouds of Glory': The Near-Death Experiences of Western Children and Teens," in Holden, J. M., Greyson, B. and James, D. (eds) *The Handbook of Near-Death Experiences: Thirty Years of Investigation*. Santa Barbara: Praeger/ABC-CLIO, pp. 87-107.

Talwar, V. and Lee, K. (2008) "Social and Cognitive Correlates of Children's Lying Behavior." *Child Development*, vol. 79, no. 4, pp. 866-881.

Tassell-Matamua, N. and Murray, M. (2014) "Near-Death Experiences: Quantitative Findings from an Aotearoa New Zealand Sample." *Journal of Near-Death Studies*, vol. 33, no.

1, pp. 3-29.

"The Day I Died! My Near Death Experience!" (2010) YouTube video, added by Kelli In The Raw [Online]. Available at www.youtube.com/watch?v=_lfpxaGMNUs (Accessed 15 November 2013).

The Day I Died: The Mind, the Brain, and Near-Death Experiences (2002). Directed and Produced by Kate Broome. [videorecording]. London, UK: British Broadcasting Corporation.

The divine Love we share between us is all that truly matters and is measured and endures (2020) *The divine Love we share between us is all that truly matters and is measured and endures* [Online]. Available at iands.org/research/nde-research/nde-archives31/newest-accounts/1478-the-divine-love-we-share-between-us-is-all-that-truly-matters-and-is-measured-and-endures.html (Accessed 24 September 2020).

"The Life Review" (2014) YouTube video, added by Nanci Danison [Online]. Available at www.youtube.com/watch?v=RTGQ6Wmha8U (Accessed 29 August 2015).

Thonnard, M., Charland-Verville, V., Brédart, S., Dehon, H., Ledoux, D., Laureys, S. and Vanhaudenhuyse, A. (2013) "Characteristics of Near-Death Experiences Memories as Compared to Real and Imagined Events Memories." *PLoS ONE*, vol. 8, no. 3, e57620 [Online]. DOI: 10.1371/journal.pone.0057620 (Accessed 1 May 2018).

van Lommel, P. (2010) *Consciousness Beyond Life: The Science of the Near-Death Experience*. New York: HarperOne.

van Lommel, P., van Wees, R., Meyers, V. and Elfferich, I. (2001) "Near-death Experience in Survivors of Cardiac Arrest: A Prospective Study in the Netherlands." *The Lancet*, vol. 358, no. 9298, pp. 2039-2045.

Voss, R. S., Helgen, K. M. and Jansa, S. A. (2014) "Extraordinary Claims Require Extraordinary Evidence: A Comment on Cozzuol et al. (2013)." *Journal of Mammalogy*, vol. 95, no. 4, pp. 893-898.

W., Martin (2017) "Martin W NDE 8303", *Near-Death Experience Research Foundation*, 10 June [Online]. Available at www.nderf.org/Experiences/1martin_w_nde.html (Accessed 15 February 2020).

"What is the meaning of life? - Near Death Experience - of Wayne Morrison" (2014) YouTube video, added by NDE Accounts - Afterlife Stories [Online]. Available at www.youtube.com/watch?v=vw6W_gopaHM (Accessed 8 August 2014).

Wright, S. (2018) *Knowledge Transmission*. New York: Routledge.

Zingrone, N. L. and Alvarado, C. S. (2009) "Pleasurable Western Adult Near-Death Experiences: Features, Circumstances, and Incidence," in Holden, J. M., Greyson, B. and James, D. (eds) *The Handbook of Near-Death Experiences: Thirty Years of Investigation*. Santa Barbara: Praeger/ABC-CLIO, pp. 17-40.

ACADEMIC AND SPECIALIST

Iff Books publishes non-fiction. It aims to work with authors and titles that augment our understanding of the human condition, society and civilisation, and the world or universe in which we live.
If you have enjoyed this book, why not tell other readers by posting a review on your preferred book site.
Recent bestsellers from Iff Books are:

Why Materialism Is Baloney
How true skeptics know there is no death and fathom answers to life, the universe, and everything
Bernardo Kastrup
A hard-nosed, logical, and skeptic non-materialist metaphysics, according to which the body is in mind, not mind in the body.
Paperback: 978-1-78279-362-5 ebook: 978-1-78279-361-8

The Fall
Steve Taylor
The Fall discusses human achievement versus the issues of war, patriarchy and social inequality.
Paperback: 978-1-78535-804-3 ebook: 978-1-78535-805-0

Brief Peeks Beyond
Critical essays on metaphysics, neuroscience, free will, skepticism and culture
Bernardo Kastrup
An incisive, original, compelling alternative to current mainstream cultural views and assumptions.
Paperback: 978-1-78535-018-4 ebook: 978-1-78535-019-1

Framespotting
Changing how you look at things changes how
you see them
Laurence & Alison Matthews
A punchy, upbeat guide to framespotting. Spot deceptions and
hidden assumptions; swap growth for growing up. See and be free.
Paperback: 978-1-78279-689-3 ebook: 978-1-78279-822-4

Is There an Afterlife?
David Fontana
Is there an Afterlife? If so what is it like? How do Western ideas
of the afterlife compare with Eastern? David Fontana presents
the historical and contemporary evidence for survival of physical
death.
Paperback: 978-1-90381-690-5

Nothing Matters
a book about nothing
Ronald Green
Thinking about Nothing opens the world to everything by
illuminating new angles to old problems and stimulating new
ways of thinking.
Paperback: 978-1-84694-707-0 ebook: 978-1-78099-016-3

Panpsychism
The Philosophy of the Sensuous Cosmos
Peter Ells
Are free will and mind chimeras? This book, anti-materialistic
but respecting science, answers: No! Mind is foundational to all
existence.
Paperback: 978-1-84694-505-2 ebook: 978-1-78099-018-7

Punk Science
Inside the Mind of God
Manjir Samanta-Laughton
Many have experienced unexplainable phenomena; God, psychic abilities, extraordinary healing and angelic encounters. Can cutting-edge science actually explain phenomena previously thought of as 'paranormal'?
Paperback: 978-1-90504-793-2

The Vagabond Spirit of Poetry
Edward Clarke
Spend time with the wisest poets of the modern age and of the past, and let Edward Clarke remind you of the importance of poetry in our industrialized world.
Paperback: 978-1-78279-370-0 ebook: 978-1-78279-369-4

Readers of ebooks can buy or view any of these bestsellers by clicking on the live link in the title. Most titles are published in paperback and as an ebook. Paperbacks are available in traditional bookshops. Both print and ebook formats are available online. Find more titles and sign up to our readers' newsletter at http://www.johnhuntpublishing.com/non-fiction
Follow us on Facebook at https://www.facebook.com/JHPNonFiction
and Twitter at https://twitter.com/JHPNonFiction